Philosophical Anthropology: Selected Chapters

UNI SLOVAKIA series
Volume 9

Philosophical Anthropology: Selected Chapters

Jana Trajtelová

Bibliographic Information published by the Deutsche Nationalbibliothek

The Deutsche Nationalbibliothek lists this publication in the Deutsche Nationalbibliografie; detailed bibliographic data is available in the internet at http://dnb.d-nb.de

The publication of this book is part of the project Support for Improving the Quality of Trnava University (ITMS code 26110230092) — preparation of a Liberal Arts study program, which was supported by the European Union via its European Social Fund and by the Slovak Ministry of Education within the Operating Program Education. The text was prepared at the Department of Philosophy, Faculty of Philosophy, Trnava University in Trnava.

Design and Layout: © Jana Sapáková, Layout JS.
Printing: VEDA, Publishing House of the Slovak Academy of Sciences

ISSN 2366-2697
ISBN 978-3-631-67462-8
E-ISBN 978-3-653-06648-7
DOI 10.3726/978-3-653-06648-7

© Peter Lang GmbH
Internationaler Verlag der Wissenschaften
Frankfurt am Main 2016

All rights reserved.

Peter Lang Edition is an Imprint of Peter Lang GmbH.
Peter Lang – Frankfurt am Main · Bern · Bruxelles · New York · Oxford · Warszawa · Wien

All parts of this publication are protected by copyright. Any utilisation outside the strict limits of the copyright law, without the permission of the publisher, is forbidden and liable to prosecution. This applies in particular to reproductions, translations, microfilming, and storage and processing in electronic retrieval systems.

This publication has been peer reviewed.

www.peterlang.com

Contents

Introduction		7
1.	What is Philosophical Anthropology?	11
2.	The Human Place in the Cosmos	25
3.	A Rational Animal?	39
4.	Culture	51
5.	The Issue of Freedom	61
6.	The Person and the Constitutive Dynamics of Interpersonal Relationships	75
7.	Appendix: Short Exercise Book and Closing Remarks	93
Bibliography		97

Introduction

Emmerich Coreth, the Austrian philosopher, opened the question of man in terms of philosophical anthropology, by saying that no other known living creatures ask questions about their existence, their essence, or their place and meaning in the world: "Only man asks questions; he questions everything, even himself, his essence – exceeding the immediacy of what is given, heading to the very foundations" (Coreth, 1994, p. 10). In the 20th century, the philosophical question of man experienced a rebirth. While trying to consistently examine the ontological structure of a human being from a philosophical point of view, Max Scheler, the founder of modern philosophical anthropology, questioned specifically "man's place in the universe"; Martin Buber raised the philosophical "problem of man", and Emerich Coreth summarised the point of philosophical and anthropological research through Kant's simple question: "What is man?". Many other contemporary thinkers have declared their allegiance to philosophical inquiry known as **philosophical anthropology**. Many other authors with various scholarly concerns, such as E. Cassirer or K. Lorenz, have spoken directly of their contribution to the philosophical-anthropological issue. Since their very beginnings, philosophical as well as religious thinking have mused upon the origin and essence of man, his or her destiny, and the meaning of his or her existence. M. Landmann made an apt comment on the issue by saying that every *anthropos* is *already* an anthropologist (Landmann, 1982, p. 10). It seems that the lot of man really is to question and learn restlessly, first of all, about his own being.

What does the uniqueness of reflections in philosophical anthropology consist of? A person within a peculiar cultural and historical context directly or indirectly always *already* cognises and interprets himself or herself on the basis of various theological or philosophical traditions and today especially on the basis of ever increasing knowledge of natural and social sciences. What is the focused philosophical thematisation of the issue of man in philosophical anthropology good for? Philosophical anthropology seeks to provide the unifying philosophical perspective on the meaning of a human being as *always* and *already* an integrated *whole* and *unity* of his or her specific anthropological attributes, that is to say that absolutising only one of them may lead to reductions with serious existential consequences.

This auxiliary textbook is a thematisation and systematisation of **selected key topics and issues** of philosophical anthropology. Since we believe that the issue of man cannot be grasped through only one characteristic or attribute (as an exhaustively qualified "human essence"), the chapters of this text attempt to introduce more various constitutive fundamental aspects which essentially characterize human beings (rationality, formation of culture, freedom, person, interpersonality), which, however, are cumulated and converged into the reflections on man as a *unique personal being*; only within this unifying personalistic perspective may the particular anthropological aspects reveal their authentic sense. We introduce an overview of selected philosophical-anthropological topics, influential persons and writers related to these, and methodological influences and approaches. The textbook is primarily intended for bachelor students of philosophical anthropology – to make selected key issues more transparent and accessible to them, to lead and refer them to deeper involvement in philosophical anthropological studies. Although the systematic works and textbooks of philosophical anthropology are very helpful, only the original texts and more intense self-study (see "Recommended literature") can help students grasp the issue thoroughly. To every chapter we have assigned a task which is formulated thematically; it is to be a creative activity for the student – involving the original texts of philosophical anthropology, as well as implementing it "into life" through philosophical and anthropological reflections of films or literary works. At the end of the textbook, students may test their knowledge in the short concluding questions section.

1. What is Philosophical Anthropology?

Philosophical anthropology –pre-understanding – anthropinum
– homo sapiens – unity of man

Philosophical anthropology is a systematic philosophical examination of the question "What is man?". The etymology we know leads us to an analogous definition. The Greek words *anthropos* and *logos* may be translated as *human being* and *reason* (as well as *word, meaning*); therefore, a simplified definition may be that philosophical anthropology is a **philosophical theory on man**. A human individual questions his or her identity – 1) as a member of the Homo sapiens species, 2) in terms of his or her historical and social identity and, most of all, 3) in terms of his or her unique personal identity.

From the very beginning, differences in the understanding of the concept of philosophical anthropology should be noted:

1) Philosophical anthropology as an integral part of philosophical thinking
2) Philosophical anthropology as an independent philosophical discipline of the 20th century

In the former case, we address philosophical anthropology supposing that every philosophy always, implicitly or explicitly, brings its own anthropology. Examining the philosophical schools of all history of philosophy, we would conclude with respective **philosophical and anthropological models of man** (which is also true in a wider scope, of course, within the framework of theology and mythological ideas, too). Therefore, we can speak of Platonic, Aristotelian, Thomistic, Cartesian, personalist, existentialist anthropology, etc. Concerning the teaching of philosophical anthropology, many publications traditionally begin with an overview of the basic philosophical and anthropological ideas in the history of philosophy, or more broadly, in the history of thought, which have shaped the further development of thinking about a man (Letz, 2011, pp. 13 – 36; Šlosiar, 2002, pp. 11 – 84; Coreth, 1994, pp. 20 45; Gálik, 2008, pp. 11 – 92). We will mention some of them as part of our systematic approach, rather than chronologically[1]. Primal areas of

---

[1] We suppose that the student has a sufficient knowledge of the history of philosophy and of the philosophical conceptions of man and relatively.

man's self-interpretation are, undoubtedly, myths and religions, later also philosophy, art and literature.

Philosophical anthropologies have various types of classifications, e.g. according to their methodological aspects and the peculiar nature of philosophical conceptions (rational – irrational, metaphysical – scientistic, objectivistic – subjectivistic, etc.) or according to their fundamental ontological insights (naturalistic and materialistic, and personalistic and spiritualistic) (Kowalczyk, 1991, p. 5). J. Letz offers another type of the classification of philosophical anthropologies: vitalistic types (e.g. W. Dilthey, H. Bergson and others), existential types (e.g. G. Marcel, J. Jaspers), personalistic types (e.g. M. Buber, M. Scheler), phenomenological-ontological types (e.g. A. Gehlen, A. Portmann), existential and transcendental-thomistic types (e.g. E. Coreth, K. Wojtyla), and nature-scientistic-evolutionary types (e.g. P.T. de Chardin, C. Tresmontant) (Letz, 2011, p. 22 – 36).

E. Coreth states that philosophical thinking itself has always inevitably been "anthropologically determined by its origin and objective" (Coreth, 1994, p. 21). A man is always the one asking questions; he or she asks them in his or her specific human way, in line with his or her possibilities and way of perception; thus, it is impossible to separate knowledge of the world from self-cognition. It is also obvious that each period of history brings some answers on the basis of its own contexts – in accordance with its form of specific self-awareness. This experience of history implies that the image of a man has no steady form; it has been developing and changing, even though the way of questioning and its existential dimension may be described as anthropologically constant. Thus, a man, making an issue of himself or herself through philosophical reflection, never starts "out of nothing". Somehow he or she always understands what "man" (and "who am I") means; therefore, when researching, we cannot avoid the so-called hermeneutic circle of the always present initial pre-understanding (Coreth, 1994, pp. 14 – 16): *"An a priori horizon forms the precondition for the possibility of the performance of questioning."* "Man" remains an "open question" – both at the individual as well the social level of knowledge.

By the latter we mean philosophical anthropology as a peculiar **philosophical school**, or in a wider sense, a line of philosophical reflections and research on man working for the more *holistic* grasp. This philosophical movement originated in Germany in the early 20th century, and was often referred to as a modern "anthropological turn". Max Scheler (1874 – 1928) has been traditionally considered its "father". In 1928 two key philosophical-anthropological works were issued in Cologne: Scheler's *The Human Place in the Cosmos (Die Stellung des Menschen im Kosmos)*, and Helmuth Plessner's, *The*

Levels of the Organic and Man (Die Stufen des Organischen und der Mensch). Philosophical anthropology questions the essence of man, i.e. *what* makes human a human, or *through what* is a human a human. It tries to bring an "essential definition" of man, thus grasp the "something" which defines us essentially – a kind of *essential* function or aspect.

Michael Landmann states that the arising of philosophical anthropology is accompanied and influenced by these factors: refusal of positivism and all types of reductionism, dissatisfaction with traditional theories of knowledge and increasing necessity of the establishment of an independent ontological region of man (Holzhey, Röd, 2006, pp. 287 – 288).

In this context, a new **methodology** was developed, merging three key approaches: 1) Philosophical anthropology refuses to examine a man only in the light of tradition, although it reflects many traditional theological and philosophical concepts of man and engages with them seriously. 2) Philosophical anthropology authors respond to the expansion of special scientific research, they study and reflect on the contemporary knowledge of natural and social sciences, and try to creatively integrate them into the holistic philosophical image of a man (biology, physiology, evolutionary sciences, ethology, empirical psychology and sociology, ethnography, theories of culture, religious studies, etc.) 3) The phenomenological method became the basic approach of philosophical anthropology authors who themselves voiced their support for phenomenology and its specific method. The question "What is man" is, in fact, a phenomenological question about an "essence" or "eidetic structures" (Holzhey, Röd, 2006, s. 293). A perspective of the first person, phenomenological epoché, precise description of the "how" of experience, the search for essential structures of experience and the constitution of meaning – all of these are the precious philosophical tools handed down to 20th century philosophers by the founder of phenomenology, E. Husserl (1859 – 1938). Thus, philosophical anthropology grasps a man through a so-called first *and* third person experience – phenomenologically and critically in the very midst of traditional philosophical, theological or contemporary scientific concepts.

Leading philosophical anthropology authors (Max Scheler, Helmuth Plessner, and Arnold Gehlen) draw primarily from man's place in nature as the biological sciences find it – side by side with other living creatures. They ask: What does the uniqueness of a man, our unique place in nature consist in? What distinguishes humans from animals? More precisely, what is the core of the unique human specificity – anthropinum – defining a human person *as a human person*? The primarily biological orientation of the beginning of philosophical anthropology was asking about the comparison of man and animal, or in a broader sense, about man's position in the whole of the organic world. In the 1920's, philosophical anthropology was heavily influenced by e.g. anthropologically important research by P. Alsberg, L. Bolek, and Jakob von Uexküll (Holzhey, Röd, 2006, pp. 290-292). Alsberg pointed out that human development has been determined by "the principle of body release using artificial tools", i.e. the development and implementation of tools (material, linguistic, conceptual) allowed a man to distance from nature and develop (even in a sense of physical adaptation) in a specific human way (Holzhey, Röd, 2006, pp. 290-292). Uexküll significantly contributed to the discussion by his exploration of binding of specific animal species to their own distinctive environments. The most discussed unique aspect defining a human being as specifically human became a "spiritual dimension" (Scheler) including the sphere of culture (Plessner, Gehlen), exceeding the pure biological indisputability we share with the rest of the living world (including simple vegetative functions as well as practical intelligence) (also see Sokol, 2002, pp. 23-31).

Philosophical anthropology authors have also been united in their effort to understand a man **holistically,** i.e. as an integrated **unity** of various unique aspects or spheres of being, i.e. according to the manners in which man *experiences* himself *as* a biologic, sensual, rational, emotional, as well as cultural, spiritual and social being. In his extensive work, Scheler revealed and examined the individual dimensions of human experience in a great detail; Coreth noted three specific ways of human self-realisation (spiritual knowing, volition and action); Cassier discerned unique spheres of sense giving, which he defined as distinctive symbolic forms (a myth, religion, science, art, etc.). The criticism of absolutising a partial view on a human being via specialised sciences (not the criticism of science itself and its progressing areas of research) or partial aspects in general (a person as a *mere* rational, social, historical, etc. being) was reflecting on the failure of naturalism when it comes to a human person which is *always* and *already* a *complex integrated personal unity or whole* (Coreth, 1994, p. 16; Buber, 1997, p. 18). This has been nicely expressed by G. Marcel: "A being whose deepest originality consists, perhaps, not only in enquiring into the nature of things, but in questioning himself, about his own essence is, by this very fact, situated beyond all the partial replies in which such an enquiry can issue" (Marcel, 2003, p. 129).

How do particular fields of science work? They select a specific area of human reality which is then examined by their own methodology – from a very specific, focused point of view. Then they rightly claim accuracy and exactness. However, they necessary ignore those aspects which are not relevant for the research or the aspects they cannot grasp through their methods; they abstract from the concrete for the sake of generally applicable conclusions. Therefore, philosophical anthropology reminds this to be the reason why none of the partial sciences can grasp the whole of human reality; however, they can significantly contribute to our understanding of it. Moreover, a man (one of his or her aspects) is necessarily objectified; a human person is the object of examination as an object among other objects. This is, of course, not only legitimate, but also necessary way of approach within objective scientific research. However, Husserl already pointed out the insufficient uncritical accepting of proliferating facts of the empirical sciences and positivism, generally speaking of a crisis of science and philosophy as well as European culture. According to him, the crisis is predominantly rooted in the objectivism started by Galileo's mathematisation of nature, causing a reduction of human cognition to a mathematical (scientific) model only, which became the paradigm in all other research fields, including the contemporary research of subjectivity – empirical psychology (Husserl, 1996, p. 27). Science resigned from answering the basic questions of human existence; it became rather a storehouse of facts (Zvarík, 2011, p. 58). It is no coincidence that Husserl's method became the leading method of philosophical anthropological inquiry.

In related issues, S. Kowalczyk names three exemplary types of reductionism, significantly reducing the idea of man, leading to determinism and limiting his or her own self-understanding and self-actualisation. They include "biologism" and "physicialism" corresponding to the mechanistic-materialistic model of man, while man is interpreted on the basis of our regular biological and physico-chemical processes and reduced to them; "psychologism" reducing the human being and self-experience to the principles of his or her psychological processes; a typical example of this is Freud's or Skinner's model of man; and finally "sociologism" (e.g. Marxism), where man is understood as a product of society and a result of social, cultural and economic relationships to which he or she is perfectly subjected. (Kowalczyk, 1991, pp. 7-14). Philosophical anthropology authors, in the times of Scheler as well as today, like philosophers of many other schools of the day (e.g. personalism, existentialism), responded to these tendencies to reductionism and its possible wide-ranging implications; they perceived the need for a new philosophical approach – hereinbefore exemplarily interpreted by Husserl.

Eventually, it is necessary to explain the relation of philosophical anthropology and **anthropological sciences**, or anthropology as understood by the contemporary language usage of the broader academic community. In a wider scholarly context, the word anthropology mostly refers to the sciences of a human person (as an individual of the *Homo sapiens* species), researching his or her biological as well as cultural nature (*biological* anthropology and *cultural* anthropology as two basic anthropological scientific disciplines). Therefore, anthropologists refer to a human person as a *two-dimensional being* – as a *bio-cultural being* equally subjected to the laws of nature as well as to the structure and influence of culture (Soukup, 2005, p. 13).[2] This distinction is well-known in the reflections of philosophical anthropology philoso-

---

2   The broad spectrum of anthropology may be demonstrated by the example of the division method of anthropological sciences in North America. In the North American context, anthropology is understood as composed of four key scientific disciplines: *archaeology, anthropological linguistics, biological (of physical) anthropology and cultural anthropology (or ethnology)*. They define anthropology as a social science concerning science as well as classic humanities. All of these areas have been standard and stable pillars of anthropological explorations in many world university and specialist institutions. In Europe, a tendency to preserve standard classification of knowledge and sciences within the science and social science disciplines with their subject areas and methodology prevails. Nowadays, so-called *applied anthropology* should be among the standard anthropological disciplines, too. Within its framework, anthropological knowledge has been practically used to deal with intercultural issues, e.g. in the field of healthcare or economic development, like in the case of various environmental and anti-discrimination activities (Trajtelová, 2013, pp. 13-26).

phers, too. Philosophical anthropology, however, is not directly a part of established anthropological research, but rather an independent philosophical discipline integrating the knowledge acquired from special anthropological sciences, critically and philosophically considering that knowledge and, on its basis, bringing forward a comprehensive philosophical model of a person.

Stanislav Kowalczyk tried to create a general classification of existing anthropological disciplines according to the nature of the subject focus – into four main types which are presented at the end of the chapter, since we consider them a purposeful systematisation of anthropologically oriented research. We distinguish these types as: 1) natural anthropology; 2) cultural (social) anthropology – both of a primarily factual, exact, descriptive character, based on special scientific research; 3) theological anthropology (based on Revelation); and 4) philosophical anthropology – focused on rational critical reflections on an issue, and including evaluation-prescriptive elements (Kowalczyk, 1991, p. 7).

Task:

Select and carry out one of the following tasks:

1. Write a free philosophical essay (5-7 standard pages) on the topic "Man as a Philosophical Problem", using at least three relevant philosophical sources.

2. Write a philosophical reflection (5-7 standard pages) on the movie, *The Elephant Man* (David Lynch, 1980), focusing on the philosophical-anthropological question "What is man?" When writing free reflections, use relevant philosophical literature.

Recommended literature:

(for recommended English sources consult your teacher)
GÁLIK, S.: *Filozofická antropológia. Porozumenie človeka z hľadiska „filozofie večnosti"*. Bratislava: Iris, 2008.[3]
RÖD, W. – HOLZHEY, H.: Filosofická antropologie. In: *Filosofie 19. a 20. storočia II.* Praha: Oikoymenh, 2006, pp. 287-322.
ŠLOSIAR, J.: *Od antropologizmu k filozofickej antropológii*. Bratislava: Iris, 2002.

---

[3] *Philosophische Anthropologie. Erster und Zweiter Teil.* (= *Neuen Anthropologie.* Band 6 u. 7). hrsg. von Hans-Georg Gadamer und Paul Vogler. Georg Thieme Verlag, Stuttgart 1974/1975; GERHART ARLT: *Philosophische Anthropologie.* Metzler, Stuttgart 2001; M. TILES: *Philosophical Anthropology.* In: Encyclopædia Britannica. 1989.

2. The Human Place in the Cosmos

Max Scheler – the essence of man – sublimation – vital impetus – spirit

The fundamental text of philosophical anthropology is the text by the phenomenologist, Max Scheler (1874 – 1928) – *The Human Place in the Cosmos (Die Stellung des Menschen im Kosmos, 1928)*. It may not be great in size, but it is a rich text. Therefore, we have decided to introduce Scheler at the beginning, as he well defines specific philosophical attempts at philosophical anthropology. The text was originally given as a lecture in 1927 in Darmstadt, reflecting on a special man's standpoint in the world. He based his reflections on contemporary knowledge and discoveries of biological morphology and the research of animal behaviour and plant life. Scheler tried to grasp man holistically – by inquiring into his relation to nature and defining his special position in it.

Firstly, Scheler distinguished between two meanings of the word "human": 1) human as a biological being with a fixed place in the natural animal life scheme (he is on the top of the range of vertebrates and mammals), and 2) human as a being with a seemingly peculiar and unique place in the world; this cannot be compared to the status of any other creatures. In this sense, Scheler assumes a specific *essence of man* (Scheler, 1968, p. 45).

Scheler draws attention to the fact that we have come to a stage in history, when there is no "unified idea of man" that would be accepted generally (contrary to e.g. the Middle Ages). Instead, he introduces three paradigms of anthropological thinking – three different models of human self-explanation in the history of the West. Scheler says that if one were to ask an educated European what he thought, when confronted with the word "man," three disparate ideological views would start competing with each other. (Scheler, 1968, p. 44). They are:

1) Judeo-Christian (Biblical) view of man (based on the religious faith, Revelation)
2) Greek-ancient view of man (philosophy – man as a rational animal)
3) Scientific view (science – man as a product of evolutionary natural processes).

Scheler calls for the search of the unified view of man which cannot be confused with a theory about man. "The essence of man is in no sense abstract or arbitrary;

the essence of man is concretely evident, immediately and directly, as a lived totality open to multiple modes and manners of concretization, manifestation, or presence. The complexity and richness of this essence is deepened profoundly when the phenomenon is seen as it *is*, concretized in a unique personal life, which life is integral to life with other persons in this universe." (Luther, 1974, p. 3).

To understand Scheler's conclusions concerning the essence and place of man in the world, we will first explain the broader context of his thought. As a phenomenologist, he was building on the *experience* of man with himself as he exists in the world as well as with the world. Human experience is trustworthy and self-evident. It is the only original source and a legitimate basis of all knowledge, including the scientific one. How am I given to myself in my experience? How is the world given to me in my experience? Experience innocently gives to us what is *as it is* – directly, fully and evidently. And this has to be true in the case of the phenomenon of "man", too. We always encounter already the *whol*e and each phenomenon is in *relation* to all other phenomena. The fullness of my present experience is only a perspective or an aspect of any possible experience of being. The *whole* may be precisely encountered in and through perspectives characterised by their own internal completeness, richness and perfection; „lived experiencing is always an experiencing of a whole or the totality from a certain perspective." (Luther, 1974, pp. 2-3). Each phenomenon, as well as each dimension of being is a part of the whole of being and only in the context of the whole may its true meaning be revealed.

However, each phenomenon and dimension of being is also given independently, or possibly it may be abstracted from the whole of being and made a subject of phenomenological inquiry. This is what Scheler did in the sum of his extensive work: he examined various *dimensions* of human experience to understand the whole of human reality. Thus, the gateway to knowledge is an *openness* and *attention* to phenomena; this is equally useful to philosophers as well as to scientists. And this is the way the *world* is, obviously, given to us in its original sense through our original experience: as a multi-layered richly-structured *unity*. And a *person* also reveals himself or herself in a network of very complex ontological relations. Reality, given as unity in its fullness and inexhaustible richness, is of a relational nature (Luther, 1974, pp. 2-3).

First of all, an **inorganic level** of reality is given as force centres, blind forces and concentrated energies (e.g. lightning, earthquakes, hardness of minerals, splitting the atom, etc.). It is a unique richly structured sphere of microscopic and macroscopic events and processes of the natural world, ruled by its own internal structural laws. It is characterised by the absence of interiority and individuality. This fundamental natural blind pressure or force – "**Drang**" (urge, drive) – is thus active in an inorganic level of reality and is demonstrated within and through it. However, it is the same kind of primordial drive or thrust which will be later found in the sphere of the organic world, too, in a specific way as a vital impetus, "Lebensdrang" (see below).

The **organic sphere** of being is demonstrated as a blind life force, "**Lebensdrang**", the ceaseless movement of life or vital urge tending to relief and actualize itself. The stunning richness and diversity of living forms has been manifested as unity of life in multiplicity. Within this, interiority occurs as a new internal "dimension" of reality. It is characterised by a kind of directedness toward a purpose (life support, growth, development, proliferation). A vital impetus has two main "objectives" (as Freud noted – Eros and Thanatos): a maximum realization and reproduction and a maximum restriction and death. (Luther, 1974, p. 10-12). Inorganic and organic spheres have been primarily experienced as resistance (also Patočka, 1968, p. 28).

Now we will proceed with the description of a specific person's place in the whole of existence. It certainly belongs to the organic sphere of being and to a quite unique manifestation of *Lebensdrang*. When searching for the essence of man, Scheler started with searching for the hierarchy of the "psychic", i.e. vital forms, forms of the organic world. He identified the psychic with the phenomenon of the life itself. In his *The Human Place in the Cosmos,* he distinguished four levels of psychical life – four vital principles or four "essential forms of soul" (*Wesensformen*): impulsive emotions, instinct, habitual behaviour, and practical intelligence. While more complex life forms always include the less complex.

1) The lowest level of the psychic life form is typical of plant life. As "psychic proto-phenomenon" it represents an unconscious life force without perceptions and impressions. Plant existence is, thus, actualized through its growth, nourishment, reproduction, and finally its extinction. This unconscious vital urge is also present in animals and people as the lowest component of their psychic life. "In animals and man the vital impetus is identified further as a complex of instinct, habit, and practical intelligence, all of which indicate an increasing specificity and specialization of it." (Luther, 1974, p.9).

2) **Instincts** are innate schemes and behaviour dispositions playing the most important role in the survival of individuals and species preservation (e.g. a way of nourishment, reproduction, or self-preservation). Instinct, being innate, is always bound to a species and beneficial for the species. It is characterised by

a "rigidity", "readiness" and fixity of structure and function (in comparison to the other life forms noted below). It defines the precise way in which an animal reacts to its environment, to which it is specifically bound. It also brings along a typical behaviour specialisation characterising the given species (not an individual). It is a decisive element of animal behaviour its world: "What an animal can see and hear is only what is of importance to its instincts" (Scheler, 1968, p. 53).

3) Instinctive behaviour, however, enables the discovery of two other, qualitatively superior, principles of living organisms typical of two new behaviours: "habitual" and "intelligent". **Habitual behaviour**, related to the associative memory operations and functioning of the conditioned reflexes, enables some release from the rigidity of instinct, since an animal can learn through practice. Animals are able to form new associations, e.g. through a "trial-and-error" method; thereby they can adapt to specific conditions and repeated stimuli from their environment, and react to them respectively. In the case of humans, the principle of association and reproduction (learning, accepting cultural models) is an important forming element, in a specific human form generationally also related to the emergence and development of *tradition* (Scheler, 1968, p. 59).

4) **Practical intelligence** allows an animal to cope with even brand new situations – individually, purpose-

fully, "creatively" and without any prior attempts (like the "intelligent" behaviour of some chimpanzees and their inventiveness in new situations). "Discovery" or resolving a difficulty within the given situation is "sudden" ("Aha!" experience). Practical intelligence, too, belongs, according to Scheler, to an organically bound domain; it is always purposeful, related to a specific situation and a vital goal. It is also linked to the (organically bound) ability to choose (e.g. to decide between individuals when mating).

Finally, Scheler asks: If animals are able to behave intelligently on the basis of thinking processes, what is the difference between a human person and an animal? Is there any *essential* difference at all? (Scheler, 1968, p. 65).

In Scheler's opinion, what we as people have "more" is not only another (higher) level in the hierarchy of life forms. *Drang* and *Lebensdrang* are not the only ontological principles of reality; the full picture is much more dynamic, much more complex. No doubt, all of the above mentioned vital principles qualify man as a part of nature. However, what places him above nature, quite specifically and essentially, is a principle **contradictory** to movement of life – **spirit.**

Eventually, Scheler describes a human being as an ontological encounter and complementary interaction

(Luther, 1974) of two principles – "***Lebensdrang***" and "***Geist***" (spirit) which is much different from the movement of life; it is contradictory. Only in human existence, in the process of "becoming" a person *as* a person, do life and spirit encounter and interact in an indissoluble unity and fruitful though tense interplay. In human existence, life has been **spiritualised** and the spirit has been **vitalised,** embodied. The dimension of freedom includes both the possibility of a person's orientation towards spiritualisation and deepening of the highest values, as well as toward "bestialisation" and the actualisation of the simplest, lowest or perverted values.

How can one recognize the presence and the work of spirit? The Greeks identified this non-vital principle as reason. Scheler ties up here but his view is much broader and complex: the activity of spirit includes all **higher intellectual, volitional and emotional acts** such as love, awe, compassion, respect, despair, free decision-making, all creative deeds and thoughts. He notes the following typical aspects or displays of spirit:

a) **Ideation** – includes the ability of objectification (while the spirit itself cannot be objectified), thinking of ideas and abstraction, or speaking more generally, it is a direct *insight into and of essences*. That is why it relates to ability to deal with formal relations in mathematics and logic, with abstracted meanings independent of specific objects, as well as with existentially significant insights of the essences of things and events (– like when Buddha, after his first encounter with a sick, then an old, then a dead man, could immediately grasp the meaning or suffering, i.e. he understood its *eidos* or essence. Thanks to the spiritual property of ideation, we grasp objects essentially, as they have sense in themselves; i.e. we are able to disregard the contingent empirical presence of an object by grasping its "essence" (e.g. for a monkey a banana is just an object for saturating its needs, but for man it is also a "fruit" of beautiful yellow colour, which a person can grow as a hobby, admire its shape, colour, beauty, thus, appreciate its value itself).

b) Thanks to the spiritual ability of ideation, a person is able to think reflexively, critically and creatively. We are the only beings in nature, which are not only conscious but conscious of our own consciousness (Plessner's ex-centricity).

c) **The spirit reveals the value** latently present in every experience. Life urge itself is value-blind. We *immediately* grasp and conceive values through peculiar spiritual acts. It happens due to our feelings and emotional life; love is the best example.

d) Spirit itself is the possibility of human **freedom** and the possibility of unfolding and developing a **personal dimension of human existence**. It seems that a person is the only creature in nature able to stand against it and say "**no**" to it; Scheler states that a person is "***Neinsagerkönner***", ascetic of life, free of immediate natural determinacy, open to the world. Human existence is not limited to the "here and now" (as life); it is virtually directed beyond nature and the world, continually **transcending** itself.

e) Man is **essentially** a personal spiritual being. Scheler defines **person** as a "center of spiritual acts" (Scheler, 1968, p. 66). The spirit manifest its presence in and as particular acts of cognitive, volitional and emotional intentions. The spirit is not "real" in the sense of the world's existence or force (Dasein, Drang), but it is real as actual (wirklich), effective in terms of concrete personal actuality (Sosain); i.e. a person *is as* thinking, wanting, suffering, hoping, loving; *as* a unique dynamic orientation of his or her spiritual acts (Luther, 1974).

The problematic as well as criticized[4] part of Scheler's model of man (i.e. of his ontological and metaphysical model of reality, too) is **the relation** of spirit and life. They have been often interpreted as mutually complementary. However, Scheler's sublimatory solution is not unambiguous; this has been proven by the passionate debates of Schelerian experts on this topic. The origi-

---

4 E.g. Martin Buber criticizes Scheler, saying that his relation of life and spirit is very obscure and it casts a new type of dualism and gnostic division on human beings (Buber, 1997, pp. 123-136).

nally *powerless spirit* **sublimates** *blind forces of life*. This way spirit uses and guides its energies toward the realisation of higher values. Scheler is inspired by and he is overcoming the Freudian term of sublimation as transformation of the lowest drives (mostly sexual) into its culturally accepted forms (like art, science).

After all, in a broader perspective of Scheler's metaphysical reflections, all of the world process consists in the mutual interaction of the originally powerless spirit and originally blind forces. The "scene" of this encounter is a man – a "partner of deity". This is the **unique human place in the cosmos.** Spirit controls the world process, directs it; the world and life urge are the performance factors of spirit. Both life and spirit are manifestations of the Ground of Being (*Weltgrund, Grund des Seins*); they are both rooted and integrated in it. Deity is a "becoming God." Thus, man cooperates in creation, man is a co-creator within the entire world process. In his earlier works, Scheler described the Ground of Being (deity, *Gottheit*) as the creative dynamic movement of eternal Loving (Luther, 1974, pp. 36-42; Luther 1972; Scheler, 1961).

Task:

Select and carry out one of the following tasks:

1. Write a philosophical reflection (5-7 standard pages) on the movie, *Diary of a Country Priest* (R. Bres-

son, 1951), focusing on the question of the relation between spirit and life forces. When writing free reflections, use relevant philosophical literature.
2. Write a philosophical essay (5-7 standard pages) on the topic, "Nature *versus* spirit? Nature *and* spirit. Nature *as* spirit?" on the basis of the motives of Jane Campion's movie, *The Piano* (1993). When writing free reflections, use suitable philosophical literature too.
3. Write a philosophical essay (5-7 standard pages) analysing the issue of the relation between life and spirit in Scheler's *Human Place in the Cosmos,* and on the basis of broader study of primary and secondary literature).

Print the paper and turn it in during the following lesson.

Recommended literature:

(for recommended English sources consult your teacher)
HODOVSKÝ, I.: Max Scheler – filosof ducha a citu. In: SCHELER, M.: *Můj filosofický pohled na svět*. Praha: Vyšehrad, 2003, pp. 9-103.[5]
SCHELER, M.: *Místo člověka v kosmu*. Praha: Academia, 1968.
SCHELER, M.: *O studu*. Praha: Mladá fronta, 1993.

---

5 SCHELER, M.: *Die Stellung des Menschen im Kosmos*. 16. Auflage. Bouvier, Bonn 2007; *Schriften zur Anthropologie*. Reclam, Ditzingen 1994; *Der Formalismus in der Ethik und die materiale Wertethik*, hrsg. von Christian Bermes, Hamburg 2014.

3. A Rational Animal?

nature – thinking – symbol – spiritual cognition – language

From the point of view of biological and evolutionary sciences, humans are an integral even though a tiny part of living nature. However, having discovered our self-consciousness, we have always rather tended to define ourselves against nature; we seem to be quite a "strange animal", as J. Sokol writes (Sokol, 2002, p. 23).

E. Coreth outlines the **specifics of human behaviour**. He adopts Scheler's notion of "man's world-openness" and summarises specific signs of human behaviour as follows:

1) The organs non-specialisation within and towards an environment becomes the biggest advantage and "specialisation" (Coreth, 1994, p. 66).
2) An insufficiency of instincts making him or her more dependent on others (a new-born child, society) and,

at the same time, later leading him or her to intellectual development and creativity (Coreth, 1994, p. 66).
3) The natural *unaccomplishment* of man as open to the world and towards others (not essentially defined merely by instinctual and developmental schemes) (Coreth, 1994, p. 66).
4) The free acting and free self-realisation (Coreth, 1994, p. 66).
5) The ability of possessing distance given by overcoming mere instinctiveness – he or she is able to objectify, grasp meaning, understand values, etc. (Coreh, 1994, p. 66).
6) Experiencing the world as "the whole of the world reality" – always and already within peculiar cultural historic social and individual contexts (Coreth, 1994, p. 66).

The so-called **essence of man** was classically defined by **thinking**, reason, and rationality ("Animal Rationale") at the dawn of western philosophy. Aristotle, in his Nicomachean Ethics (I, 13), found the principle in a person's very ability to think, which is – act rationally as well. It would be difficult to find the more obvious point differentiating humans from other animals in man's experience with him or herself and with the world. A man, who thinks, speaks, differentiates and evaluates things and events, creates unique values on this basis, and forms an ordered society and culture. Rationality is a notion used in several specific meanings, e.g. as rationality of formal-logical, scientific-theoretical thinking or as instrumental or practical rationality, leading us to meaningful and purposeful discussions. The philosophical-anthropologic definition of reason or rationality, however, must be wider. Rather, we speak of a unique person's ability of *insight into the meaning and order of being*, i.e. an ability to meaningfully, articulately and deliberately grasp the experience of himself or herself in the world and with the world (Sokol, 2004, p. 356). Rationality thus penetrates into all spheres of human existence; that is why a man simply cannot be "irrational." E. Coreth writes that even a simple sensual experience cannot be compared to the sensual experience of an animal, as the "sensory cognition of man is always experienced and understood in consciousness, already received and processed in and through thinking" (Coreth, 1994, p. 78); Similarly, E. Cassirer states that a man can relate to the world only indirectly, through the symbolic forms which characterise the functioning of human mind (Cassirer, 1977, p. 75 – 79).

Ernst Cassirer (1874-1945) of the Neo-Kantian school demonstrated that **symbolism** is a unique feature of the human cognition of reality. We grasp the world through symbolic systems. Homo sapiens are also "Homo symbolicus" – creators of the entire universe of symbolic systems. The symbol is the "key to the essence of man" (Cassirer, 1977; Cassirer, 1996).

Symbolic activity is an ever and omnipresent cognitive process producing symbols and representative signs; through these humans acquire forms for understanding the world. We can distinguish three essential symbolic forms: *language, myth, and science*. Each provides a unique approach to reality. Man "... has so enveloped himself in linguistic forms, in artistic images, in mythical symbols or religious rites that he cannot see or know anything except by the interposition of this artificial medium" (Cassirer, 1977, p. 78). He or she can no longer enter a perfectly direct relationship with nature. Human relation to the world is inevitably mediated by systems of symbols and only through them can he or she grasp and know the world. For instance, just as the relationship between a stimulus and response is absolutely direct in the case of animals, the reaction of a person reacting to a stimulus is "delayed": the response has been "hindered" by the process of **thinking**. More precisely – in the case of a functional circle of animals, the system of receptors (used by animals to receive stimuli from the outside world) and the system of effectors (responsible for the reaction to stimuli) are in close direct relation. In the case of man, there is a "third connecting link" between them – a symbolic system. This link is responsible for the unique symbolic human world – for a unique human experience represented by language, myth, religion, art, science, etc. In other words, what we call *culture*.

People have been aware that *language* is an essential attribute of humanity for a great many years. Of course, discussion about the "speech" and mutual communication of animals is still open. Cassirer admits that animals have a kind of subjective "emotional language". He draws from the well-known observations of Wolfgang Köhler who discovered that chimpanzees have relatively good verbal skills. Using gestures, they show emotional states such as fear, grief, pleading, anger, desire and joy, and even mischief. Other research of anthropoid apes by Yerkes even implied the presence of symbolic processes – as if in an early phylogenetic stage (Cassirer, 1977, p. 85). Often, the behaviour of animals does not even lack a complicated system of symbols and signals by which they respond to their surrounding physical existence. However, they lack representative signs with an objective, general sense independent of specific biological needs or practical interests. In humans, the ability of making units of sheer sense and its' relations fully independent and comprehensible – the ability of **abstraction and theoretical thinking** – has developed. Therefore, Cassirer notes that the core of the issue is the distinction between **emotional** and **predicative** language, which he understands as a "milestone between the world of animals and the world of people" (Cassirer, 1977, p. 84). The "language" of animals remains subjective and emotional. Humans have shifted from the concrete to the abstract, from the field of nature to the field of sheer meanings.

A man assigns words and concepts to objects and events and uses and understands them independently of these objects themselves. E. Coreth summarised this unique ability as the following: "The human way of thinking has an inherent ability to abstract general meaning from factual reality. Classical tradition speaks of "an abstraction", modern psychology and anthropology speak of "ideation" meaning more or less the same: an ability to abstract a certain meaning from a real particularity and to give it a general validity" (Coreth, 1994, p. 79). Using concepts, man can denote and describe various kinds of specific and ideal objects, as well as relations. We create categories and classification systems, schematically rendering and organising known reality. In the case of a baby who begins to understand the symbolism of speech, a small intellectual revolution begins (Cassirer, 1977, p. 229). Similarly, considering the historical development of human speech and research on indigenous languages, there is a generally accepted opinion on human speech being developed from more concrete world-dependent stages to the stages of ever-increasing degrees of abstraction. "The shift to general concepts and categories in the development of human speech, thus, seems very slow, but each new progress in this field leads to better orientation in the world we perceive around us; it allows us to become better acquainted with it and organise it better" (Cassirer, 1977, p. 234).

In this context, we also note, an important concept which has attracted broad professional interest in language: the discussion on **language universals** or **innate linguistic forms**. This theory is based on the thesis stating that our mind has an internal structure responsible for identification, sorting and classifying data. People possess a genetically innate "universal grammar" with language universals – universal a priori language forms. More concretely, an American linguist and philosopher, **Noam Avram Chomsky** (*1928), has noted that there are structures in our minds that are a prerequisite for grammatical speech. He, for example, draws attention to a well-known fact that children can playfully and naturally acquire language in their early childhood. He mentions the innate structure or a given prerequisite being as a basis of the possibility and form of ontogenetic language development. From this universal innate structure, all grammars of languages have derived and the child is able to "re-transform" it into a specific mode of his or her mother tongue (transformative or generative grammar). Thanks to this mechanism, children are able to differentiate between the syntactic relationships and the components of sentences, between the relation and an object, actions and agents represented by the words in a sentence; thus, they adopt language with no problems. Or in other words: the human brain should, according to Chomsky, contain a special neuron structure or an "innate module of language development" able to adopt language (Language Acquisition Device – LAD). V. Soukup notes that Chomsky's theory of the innate nature of language dispositions and structures has not only been proved by the fact that children go through the same stages of language development (even deaf children), but also by the research of **transcultural linguistics**; e.g. the fact that various languages really contain so-called "language universals" (e.g. nouns and adjectives). This theory has been very popular recently, also in the fields of other highly specialized disciplines (psycholinguistics, sociolinguistics, linguistic anthropology, cognitive science, cognitive linguistics) (Soukup, 2011, p. 147).

When searching for the essence of man, E. Coreth started with the functions significantly defining humans, being inherent and constitutive in the process of the development of our existence. He finds three specific ways of human self-realisation in the world: spiritual cognition, free volition, and morally responsible behaviour (Coreth, 1994, pp. 71 – 125).

When examining the specificity of human knowledge, Coreth systematically examines the meaning of conceptual, judging and cogitative thinking which are typical of thinking structurally. He also emphasises that **conceptual thinking** is a part of human nature itself. While a *concept* is abstract and universal, independent of time and space as well as the causal determination of physical existence, *a thing* is always concrete and particular, bound to time and space as well as to the causal events of world order; it is individual, non-interchangeable and unique. Even in these reflections, Coreth does not omit emphasising his notion of *fundamental freedom*, which pertains to humans already in a biological sense as soon as there has been release from the instinctual determinations (Coreth, 1994, p. 69). Coreth states that thanks to the **unique human ability to separate semantic content** which ceases to be directly attached to a particular thing or physical reality, in the field of thought we have relieved a space for the fundamental freedom, the freedom of thought, which is necessary for the formation and development of abstract theoretical thinking and a specifically human world (Coreth, 1994, p. 79). E. Cassirer demonstrated this fact via Helen Keller – a deaf-mute-blind girl whose world did not become fully opened in a unique human way until she understood the meaning of concept on the basis of independent and universally applicable meanings. Despite her lack of sensual data, her governess managed to lead her to this discovery, using only tactile communication (Cassirer, 1977, pp. 92 – 93).

Coreth then continues saying that from an anthropological point of view the ability of abstraction is a very important phenomenon, and allows the development of a specifically human cognition, determining the development of specifically human volition and action, which belong to the area of the spirit's freedom. We create concepts which can be fully unrelated to space-time existence (e.g. "value", "God", "law", "possibility", etc.). Thus, man is essentially different from nature as he peers above or beyond it; he or she essentially belongs to the spiritual dimension of being understood as non-material and independent of nature and its principles (Coreth, 1994, p. 83).

Regarding the **judicative reason**, we create meaningful judgements, statements; we predicate of reality. And with each statement, we claim the implicit veracity of the predication, although we may be wrong due to the restrictedness of our partial perspective. Judgement grasps reality; it claims "formal claim to unconditional validity" (Coreth, 1994, p. 84). Coreth tries to emphasise that human thought is able to speak truthfully about its world. Thinking is virtually unlimited and opened in giving judgement and if it had infinite time, it could cognise, so to say, forever. Thus, Coreth mentions the **virtual infinity** of our cognition (Coreth, 1994, p. 86). And finally, not only do we create judgements, but we are also able to process these judgements on the basis of *principles of thought* (e.g. formal logic). We draw conclusions from knowledge acquired, we state hypotheses, and create entire theoretical systems. The freedom and creativity of the human spirit seem to be limitless in the field of cognition, although just virtually, not actually.

Coreth finishes the chapter about spiritual cognition with his reflections on a non-thematised "area of proto-knowledge" which is, according to Coreth, self-evident to human cognition. He finds fundamental cognitive insights non-thematically present in every inquiry and reasoning, and they are self-evident and reliable for human cognition. This most original field of knowledge is, in his opinion, "the determining and normative basis" for all our practical and theoretical approaches to the world (Coreth, 1994, p. 83).

Task:

Select and carry out one of the following tasks.

1. Write a philosophical reflection of the given topic (5-7 standard pages) on the basis of the movie, *The Miracle Worker* (Nadia Tass, 2000). Use relevant philosophical literature.
2. Write a philosophical paper (5-7 standard pages) analysing one of the specific symbolic forms (myth, science, art, etc.) of E. Cassirer.

Recommended literature:

(For recommended English sources consult your teacher)
CASSIRER, E.: *Esej o človeku*. Bratislava: Pravda, 1977, pp. 45 – 129.
CORETH, E.: Co je člověk? Praha: Zvon, 1994.
SCHELER, M.: *Můj filozofický pohled na svet*. Praha: Vyšehrad, 2003.[6]
SOKOL, J. : *Filosofická antropologie. Člověkjako osoba*. Praha: Portál, 2002, pp. 9 – 85.

---

[6] CASSIRER, E.: *An Essay on Man: An Introduction to a Philosophy of Human Culture*. Yale University Press, 1972; *Philosophie der symbolischen Formen. (Band 1: Die Sprache, 1923; Band 2: Das mythische Denken, 1925; Band 3: Phänomenologie der Erkenntnis, 1929)*; CORETH, E.: *Was ist der Mensch?: Grundzüge einer philosophischen Anthropologie*. Innsbruck, Wien, München: Tyrolia 1973.

4. Culture

culture – act – creativity – mediated immediacy – technology

We have mentioned that in his *Essay on Man,* Ernst Cassirer considers the symbolic rational activity of a person to be the very essence of humanity (understood functionally, not substantially). This author understands his philosophy of symbolic forms not just as an epistemology, or as he says, "anthropological philosophy" or a "philosophy of man", but also as a "philosophy of culture." Man could have evolved in a specifically human way and his or her world could have acquired a specific human form, when he or she "managed" to abstract meaning and understand the sense of "symbol," i.e. when we started to use articulated speech and develop conceptual thinking – as Cassirer demonstrated, for example, through the well-known story of Helen Keller. He believes that a human being can be successfully comprehended in his or her specificity only through this symbolic "functions" (and if the "essence" of man should be mentioned, in this sense only). This specific cognitive functions are visible in the specific accomplishments of human activities, which we can call "culture": language, myth, religion, morals, law, science, i.e. all specifically human creations forming our uniquely human **cultural world** (Cassirer, 1977, p. 140). It is no coincidence that culture has become the focal point of interest of various anthropological inquiries.

Even the philosophers of modern philosophical anthropology have dealt with the phenomenon of culture seriously – as trying to grasp the specificity of man through our differentiation between humans and other animals. They qualified culture as a characteristic feature of a human being – as a tangible expression of the uniqueness of human mental and physical activity. Already in his book, *Outline of a Philosophical History of Humanity*, German philosopher **Johann Gottfried Herder** (1744-1803) regarded the cultural phenomena such as language, writing, religion, art, tradition, law, clothes or the variability of human lifestyles as the keys to human existence. Moreover, Herder stated that culture is a kind of compensation for a lack of biological equipment; it is a unique method of human adaptation to the environment (Soukup, 2011). We deal with the cultural "withdrawal" from nature – the interruption of a direct connection with the natural, which is the common denominator of philosophical anthropologists **Helmuth Plessner** (1892-1985) and **Arnold Gehlen** (1904-1976), who presents humans as **essentially cultural beings**.

The core of Plessner's teaching is the concept of **eccentricity** which he understands as a "principle of humanisation" (*The Levels of Organic and Man,* 1928). Plessner noted that every living thing mutually interacts with its environment. A plant is directly incorporated in it, all exposed to the environment and it is all "outside"; this is a so-called *open life form*. In contrast, an animal is more independent – it has its own conscious and control centre – a so-called *inclosed* and *centric life form*. It is able to control and perceive its body. A higher animal may live its life consciously, but it does not experience itself *as* conscious. According to Plessner, only a human being is characterised by a distance relation to the world and himself. We can take a distance from our own selves; we are able to objectify our own *selves*. People are self-reflective beings. Thus this twofold movement (toward and out of the conscious center) or principle of ex-centricity is a universal principle of human essence.

Ex-centricity is closely related to the creation of a specific human world, which is the world of culture, as it means a withdrawal from the implicit connection with nature. In comparison to other living creatures, **man is a creature poor in instincts**. Through ex-centricity, i.e.

as a result of a conscious reflexive ability to experience one's self, the world and the practical implications of this ability – creative and purposeful deeds – man compensates for this handicap in an "artificial" way. Yet, it should be added that the fact humans do not live from our direct natural determinacy is at the same time an anxious moment of uncertainty for us. In a reflecting distance we realise the unpredictability of an open future, our uncertain situation and vulnerability. Thus, we acquire some kind of safety "artificially": we create mediated environments, "natural artificiality", or **culture**. Plessner defined three basic anthropological laws (the law of natural artificiality, the law of mediated immediacy, and the law of utopian standpoint) (Holzhey, Röd, 2006, p. 308). E. Coreth summed them up in a single law **of mediated immediacy** (Coreth, 1994).

The philosopher and sociologist, **Arnold Gehlen,** also draws on the knowledge of biology (Gehlen, 1940). He understands philosophical anthropology as a general teaching on man which should precede all specialised anthropologies. Gehlen became known among German philosophers thanks to his work, *Man, his Nature and Place in the World,* (1940). He emphasised the holistic and systemic understanding of man whom Gehlen perceived as a unique project of nature. The starting point of his considerations is **an act, human action**. A man is an acting being able to transform nature by his or her activity and accommodate their environment. Human action does not serve only immediate biological goals and needs; it also produces something of a "higher" order – culture. Therefore, acting is, according to Gehlen, the principle making a human *a human*. The need for purposeful and creative action is, in his opinion, rooted in biological ground – as compensation for a feeble instinctive endowment.

Humans seem to be, in comparison to animals, absolutely not specialized, having just a feeble instinctive endowment and insufficient specialization of organs. Therefore, Gehlen notes that humans are **deficient beings** (*Mängelwesen*). As an impoverished animal, a person is unprotected and vulnerable to nature. **Culture** becomes a "**second nature**" for a person – a principle of "relief." Thus, man has been defined as a "naturally cultural being" (Röd, Holzhey, 2006, s. 318). An important role in cultural "relief" has been played by **speech**, being a critical breaking of immediacy, enabling communication, planning, and all action. Gehlen metaphorically calls culture "a nest" built by humans in the centre of the world. It includes **institutions** and **social norms** which should regulate the coexistence of people. Important topics of Gehlen's reflections also included technology which is an integral part of human life "in the nest". **Technology** is a unique creative act, an achievement of man, human skills and our intellect. Technology is also a unique means used by people to conquer nature. Gehlen called the world of technology "macro human" and included it among the characteristic features of human nature itself (Gehlen, 1972).

Erich Rothacker (1888–1965) and **Michael Landmann** (1913–1984) belong to the so-called cultural line of philosophic anthropology. They note that man is a product as well as a creator of culture. Landmann claims that non-specialization cannot be understood only as a cause of the development of specifically human features which should compensate for it, but it is also a consequence of this humanity itself. "Man may and even must put his specialization aside, because his life is based on a different kind of endowment. He does not need it and it could be even obstructive" (Seilerová, 1995, p. 93). To a human being Landmann assigns two basic closely interconnected characteristic signs – *freedom and creativity*. Let us mention the Renaissance thinker, Pico de la Mirandola, who perceived these two attributes as the most important and very essential aspects of a human being; through these two aspects we reach our essential nature as *imago Dei* (Seilerová, 1999, pp. 59-69). According to Landmann, creativity has been fully demonstrated by the creation of culture and the entire human world as the cultural world. And despite the variability and diversity of the historical and cultural "faces" of man, he finds this principle valid universally as the universal *anthropinum*: In any culture and historical context a person actualizes himself or herself through exercising his or her creative rational abilities, and through upbringing and training comes to be himself or herself.

An important topic related to the inquired cultural aspect is the question of the psychic unity and cultural diversity of humanity. This became crucial primarily in the area of cultural anthropology research and it has been dealt with in detail elsewhere (Trajtelová, 2013, pp. 70-80). **The principle of the psychic unity of humankind** is one of the classic anthropologic dogmas. The assumption that human nature is only one in essence, regardless of cultural and historical context, was the ground for any anthropological inquiries. Human properties and abilities and their possible development are common to all people. **Psychological universalism,** derived from the Enlightenment idea of universal rationality, became the fundamental anthropological axiom and a condition for comparative ethnographic research methods. In more contemporary language: the idea of psychical unity may be conceived as a metaphor of common hardware. **E. B. Tylor** (1832–1917), the founder of cultural anthropology, believed that despite various cultural variations, the human mind works, in principle, in the same way for all people. According to Tylor, the multiplicity of cultural variations exists due to the "**universal properties of human mind**" (Kanovský, 2004, p. 22). **James George**

Frazer (1854-1941), an important British anthropologist, was another significant follower of the idea of the psychical unity of humankind.

Franz Boas (1858-1942) markedly problematized the concept of a unified human mind. Individual cultures have their own unique direction of historical development and they cannot be evaluated by a single universal measuring tool. As the father of "historical particularism", Boas emphasised the uniqueness of each culture given by its peculiar historical development. He noted that classifications in various cultures are based on fundamentally different principles. F. Boas suggested an important distinction between **original cultural traditions** and universal **mental equipment.** The rich diversity of human cultural life forms has a primarily cultural origin. With this distinction, Boas was able to keep the concept of the fundamental unity of humankind, while defending the sovereignty of cultural and racial variations (even in the mental area).

Anthropological inter-cultural inquiries are in line with philosophical anthropologists' efforts to reveal and define the essential feature, function, or simple essence of human beings. In his paper devoted to symbolic forms of myth and religion, Cassirer noted that although individual symbolic worlds (science, myth, art) differ from each other significantly and they are largely autonomous, all of them are specifically human and have a unified and essential function ("symbolic function"), which has been specified and, so to speak, embodied in the specific areas and works of culture. "Language, art, myth and religion are not isolated, random creations. They are held together by a common bond... It is the fundamental function operating in speech, myth, art or religion which we must seek at the bottom of their innumerable shapes and utterances, and which in the last analysis we must attempt to trace back as to its common origin" (Cassirer, 1977, p. 140).

Task:

Select and carry out one of the following tasks.

1. Write a free philosophical essay (5-7 standard pages) on the topic "Man in the Age of Technology", using at least three relevant philosophical sources.
2. Write a philosophical-anthropological reflection (5-7 standard pages) on the movie, *Metropolis* (Fritz Lang, 1927), using relevant literature.
3. Considering the given issue, write a philosophical paper on the topic "Person, dialogue, culture" (5-7 standard pages) on the basis of the movie, *The Cuckoo* (A. Rogozhkin, 2002).

Print the paper and submit it in the following lesson.

Recommended literature:

(For recommended English sources consult your teacher)
GEHLEN, A.: *Duch vesvěte techniky*. Praha: Svoboda, 1972, pp. 29 - 47.
LORENZ, K.: *Osm smrtelných hříchů*. Praha: Akademia, 2001.[7]
PLESSNER, H.: Člověk jako živá bytost. In: BLECHA, I. (ed.): *Filosofická čítanka*. Olomouc: Nakladatelství Olomouc, 2000, pp. 446 -449.

---

[7] GEHLEN, A.: *Der Mensch, seine Natur und seine Stellung in der Welt*. Junker und Dünnhaupt, Berlin 1940. 3. Auflage. 1944. 4. Auflage. Athenäum-Verlag, Bonn 1950. 16. Auflage. AULA-Verlag, Wiebelsheim 2014; PLESSNER, H.: *Die Stufen des Organischen und der Mensch. Einleitung in die philosophische Anthropologie* (1928) e Gruyter; Auflage: 3. Unveränd, 1975; LOREZ, K.: *Die acht Todsünden der zivilisierten Menschheit* Piper Taschenbuch,1996.

5. The Issue of Freedom

determinism – indeterminism – compatibilism – fundamental freedom
–motivation

One of the key philosophical and anthropological issues is the question of freedom. Different possible solutions are referring to different ontological models of man. At the same time, the question expresses the existential situation of a person reflecting his or her position and possibilities within his or her being. *What is freedom?* Is just an eternal god-like desire of man, an illusion; or is it real? J. Sokol considers freedom "as one of the most characteristic features of a human being" and besides reason "as the highest attribute of man" (Sokol, 2004, p. 366). Perhaps the most intuitive definition associated with our daily lives is that freedom is the possibility to choose or the possibility to act according to one's own will. However, this definition poses another problems. What does it mean to "choose"? What is the nature of the will we tend to call "one's own"? The aim of this chapter is first to outline the issue systematically and introduce key notions and concepts. In the second part we will address the issue particularly – as it was addressed by E. Coreth.

If we pictured an imaginary line as a scale for visual illustration of the best known concepts of freedom, there would find **radical determinism concepts** on one side and the philosophical teachings of **radical freedom and indeterminism** on the other.

Sartre's radical understanding of freedom as **absolute** is a typical example of philosophical *indeterminism*. A person is absolutely free and absolutely **responsible** for his or her decisions and deeds.[8] *Determinism* (from Lat. "determinare" – to delimit, determine) is the philosophical view that everything that happens, happens inevitably, due to some kind of causality (given the relation between causes and consequences) (Sokol, 2004, p. 282); thus, the free will of a person does not exist, or possibly it is just an illusion. Everything that happens (in the material or spiritual world) has been necessarily determined in advance. Extreme forms of determin-

---

[8] "Man is condemned to be free. Condemned, because he did not create himself, yet is nevertheless free, and from the moment that he is thrown into this world he is responsible for everything he does." (Sartre, 1996, p. 24).

ism include e.g. *fatalism* (a belief in fate – just like in the Ancient myth of Oedipus), or, in terms of theism, so-called *selective predestination* (the doctrine of predestination to salvation or damnation) or determinism in a strict sense, i.e. *natural* or *causal determinism* based on the strictly given relationship between the cause and effect of natural processes. Of course, there has not just been alternative radical freedom versus necessity in the history of thought. There have been many approaches seeking some compatibility and reconciliation of deterministic and indeterministic positions – a kind of moderate determinism – a so-called philosophical **compatibilism** enabling the maintenance of a certain degree of freedom and the related concept of personal or moral **responsibility** for one's actions, which is not possible in the case of "strict" determinism (e.g. stoics, Augustine, Hobbes, Spinoza, etc.).

E. Coreth distinguished two basic types of determinism – **positivist materialism** assuming only the existence of material reality and causal necessity of physical and chemical processes (or possibly of atomic or subatomic movements,) and **idealist pantheism** in which all events are necessarily subjected to one metaphysical principle (Coreth, 1994, p. 46.).

When considering freedom, it is also important to take into account the distinction between *external* and *inter-*

nal freedom (Coreth, 1994, p. 91). **External freedom** has been understood as the freedom of volition and action not limited by any external influences (personal, political repressions, and so on.) It is, for example, the freedom of thought, conscience, religious belief, speech or a universal civil right to freedom and to live with dignity. However, external freedom does not necessarily guarantee that a person would feel free inwardly. Internal freedom means that we are not determined by anything from inside; we are not inherently pressed to choose or think in any way – even if we were bound in chains (the freedom of a prisoner or a slave.) In this spirit, Thomas Aquinas similarly distinguished "libertas a coactione", i.e. being free from external pressure and "libertas a necessitate", i.e. being free from internal necessity rooted in the nature of freedom of a person (Coreth, 1994, p. 91).

D. Palmer[9] speaks about *the concept of practical freedom,* which is guaranteed in society by laws and embraces political, economic and civil liberties, and *the concept of metaphysical freedom,* which concerns philosophy (Palmer, 2008, p. 248). The concept of metaphysical

---

9 In this chapter we largely lean on the systematisation of the problem as proposed by the American philosopher, Donald Palmer. PALMER, D.: *Does the center hold? An introduction to Western philosophy.* NY: The McGraw-Hill Companies, Inc., 2008, pp. 213-255).

freedom deals with the following philosophical theses trying to approach the concept of freedom:

1) **Absolute free will** (pure, perfect freedom) would concern just God's existence; for Palmer a free act of will would mean pursuance – that is, volition and acting (i.e. creation) would be identical. Such freedom would not be limited by anything, what brings along a difficult theological and philosophical issue (absolute freedom as arbitrariness) having been addressed also by R. Descartes in his *Mediations,* or J.-P. Sartre (two absolute wills would limit each other, therefore they could not coexist simultaneously).
2) **Relative and restricted** freedom concerns various types of compatibilisms. It grows out of the experience of a person with himself or herself in the world. The necessity to choose is our everyday experience. At the same time we experience our freedom as restricted since we make our choices within already pre-given (natural and social) conditions and options.
3) **Mental freedom** (the freedom of thought, feelings and personal attitudes) is the freedom of a slave or a political prisoner, who may be **free inwardly** despite external circumstances and who still may take his or her own stance toward situations, ideologies, etc.
4) By the term **ontological freedom,** Palmer meant a kind of freedom which has been given by our onto-

logical constitution itself. A person experiences this kind of freedom, when *experiencing the necessity of choice* between alternatives (the necessity of choice; Sartre's "condemnation" to freedom) – a choice which necessarily brings irrevocable existential consequences.

5) Finally, Palmer introduces the category of **perverse freedom** manifested by the possibility of free rejection of norms, including morality and sociality; it is a freedom of internal rebellion. It is related to the unpredictability of human deeds, with the "misusing" of freedom and "demonic freedom". The question remains whether it is a manifestation of pathology or rather of freedom in the proper sense.

Let us have a brief look at the best known forms of determinism in the history of philosophy. The first known examples of causal *mechanistic determinism* include the teachings of **Greek atomists** (Democritus, around 400 B C). Everything which exists (*to on*) is composed of atoms – an infinite number of elementary, indivisible, invisible and unchanging particles surrounded by empty space (not-existing, non-being – *me on*). They are in a constant motion which is strictly determined by trajectories prescribed by the very nature of atoms. The things of the world are created by the motion of atoms: by their collisions and merging into greater units. All movements and events inevitably happen by the "predestined" atomic trajectories. Like a soul of a person which is composed of very subtle atoms, thinking and perception are subjected to the same principle of atomic motions. It is interesting to note that this atomistic teaching was later adopted by Epicureanism (Lucretius). They seek how to maintain the freedom of choice and they come up with the *deflective theory* and the idea of randomness of atomic motion: trajectories of atoms are not given necessarily but randomly. This keeps the possibility of free thinking, a freedom of the individual's will, which itself may be the cause of the motion of things and events.

In the 18th century, among others, modern Enlightenment materialists such as **La Mettrie** (1709-1751) and **Henri d'Holbach** (1723-1789) presented exemplary theses of causal determinism. Under the influence of Newton's physics, based on a mainly mechanistic interpretation of the world, and on general applicability of natural laws, materialists believed that the same principles valid for the physical world must be equally valid for all levels of human experience (will, thought, emotions, "soul".) **Simon Laplace** (1749-1827) radicalizes the mechanism of natural causal relations, and introduces the hypothesis of such a "demon", or such an intelligence that would know all natural laws and principles perfectly, as well as all driving forces and their relations in nature. This overwhelming mind would have a perfect and full knowledge and description of the universe, the natural order in every possible moment in time – thus, it would be able to predict all future events as well as interpret the past on the basis of this all-encompassing knowledge (knowing all driving forces and the positions of all particles in the universe and the laws of their motion, i.e. the laws of classical physics.) Speaking generally, one of the fundamental principles of science since the 17th century has been the belief that nature may be explained and described in terms of causal theories, i.e. in terms of the relation between a cause and effect.

In the early 20th century, Freud's discovery of the unconscious caused a considerable stir – with regard to the debate on the freedom of a person as well. **Sigmund Freud** (1856-1939) the founder of psychoanalysis, was the first to draw attention to the unconscious level of our psychic life and its determining influence on human acts, conscious actions and choices. Similarly, in the 20th century, American psychologist, **Burrhus Frederic Skinner** (1904-1990), caused a considerable ado in the area of psychology with his work, *Beyond Freedom and Dignity*. The principles of human behaviour are decipherable; human behaviour is predictable – on the simple basis of *cause-effect*, stimulus-response mechanism. However, accepting such a radical behaviourist model of a person is accompanied by considerable practical difficulties. It challenges all functioning structures within our social order including moral and legal institutions, courts and prisons. How could we speak about moral responsibility or punishment? How could punishment be a solution, if there is no culprit, but rather a victim (of circumstances or "programming")? (Skinner, 1976, pp. 63-83). How could we speak about moral or personal responsibility in the case of a man with programmable and programmed behaviour, knowing that his or her acts are a mere result of correct or incorrect stimuli (such as upbringing, various life experience)? (Palmer, 2008, pp. 214-222).

We will now present the **personalistic solution** of transcendental neo-thomisst, Emmerich Coreth, the Austrian philosopher, as an example of a compatibilism defending free will and personal responsibility, based on a personalist view on man. In his philosophical anthropology, Coreth undertakes the phenomenological description of a human's experience with himself or herself in the world. The unique process of formation of human identity is based on specifically human cognition, willing and acting. Not only may we cognise our world, but also relate to it by our will (it offers the good, being the subject of will), and transform and adapt it creatively. We are able to objectify and embody our thoughts, visions and plans into actions.

How does E. Coreth grasp the question of freedom in this context of the creative spiritual development of a person? Coreth starts with *experience* – the experience of freedom. Every day we face choices and decisions – some of them less, some of them more existentially loaded, changing the whole orientation as well as the momentum of our existence. Many times, we experience decision-making as painful, as choosing one thing means to sacrifice another (e.g. when choosing a life partner, or, in more escalated situations, when experiencing battles of conscience and moral dilemmas, e.g. "Sophie's Choice"). Thus, we experience freedom *practically*, as the necessity of choice and decision-making, although it may be denied theoretically (and *only* theoretically – as noted by Coreth, 1994, pp. 94-95). Even the denial of freedom is an expression of our freedom: to deny freedom and accept a deterministic worldview. The real practical experience of a person in the world, however, seems to disrespect the theoretical arguments denying it. We assume this meaning of freedom when meeting other people; we base the possibility of dialogue and discussion on it, and we consider it a basis of free civil and political space.

However, according to Coreth, all of the daily *practice of choosing freely* between values, the practice of decision-making and accepting responsibility has been based on an even more original experience of freedom, called **fundamental freedom**. We can touch this freedom in several ways and it comes to existence as if at various levels of human existence. This *original non-thematic awareness of* *freedom* occurs in a person as a result of being released from immediate natural instinctual determinacy (in comparison to animals,) emerging from man's essential openness to the world.

The same human experience with freedom is that our experience is *limited*. A person gets to know himself or herself as a finite contingent being with limited, not absolute, freedom. This contingency is given *ontologically* (by the finiteness of a human being), *culturally* and *historically* (a wider social context sets the borders of free choices and acts,) and by an individual unique context of a person (by the unique scale of values adopted). This last is, however, as Coreth says, related to the authentic rational recognition of objective moral values and **ethical standards** as the real restriction of our freedom. Ethical standards and a moral relations to others are a specifically human phenomena which have been known in various forms in every age and culture. It seems that neither the thesis of "strict" determinism, nor the thesis of absolute freedom matches our daily experience.

Coreth seeks the metaphysical essence of freedom which refers to a man as a *personal* being. First, Coreth explains that if *the formal subject of reason is being as such*, then its material subject will include all richness of natural reality, which we can keep on cognising (virtually) forever. Likewise, if the *formal subject of will is the good or a value*, then its material subject includes wide range of the goods (values), from sensual to spiritual, even the Supreme Good as the ultimate goal of our desires. The problem is, however, that many times we are forced to choose between values, getting one, scarifying others. Moreover, each satisfaction is followed by a hunger for another good and an ultimate satisfaction is not in sight. Coreth distinguishes between two main types of values: the *lower values* (good-for-me) are related to the purpose and benefit of a person (pleasant, beneficial, vitally useful), and the *higher values* (good-as-such), such as moral values or the values of truth and beauty, we desire in and of themselves and we approach them naturally by a "response of appreciation" (Coreth, 1994, pp. 108-109). Correct spiritual knowledge allows us to distinguish between higher and lower values and thus to perform a proper act of preference (Scheler). Thus, it is up to our freedom, whether we choose the higher value or not. A value **motivates**, rather than determines, our choice.

I may want this or that, but I also might not want it. I even may want to want or not want not to want. We always have our good reasons or counter-reasons, motives. Experience teaches us that we are mostly able to distinguish the higher motives from the lower ones, even if the lower motives could be affecting us by a greater motivational force. We may distinguish higher motives and still choose the lower ones freely. "Motivational force rather depends on if and how... we open ourselves to the motivation of a certain value and let it influence us. The more we open ourselves, the stronger the motivation becomes and we – eventually – follow it through psychological necessity. This does not cancel freedom, but it might suggest we had freely decided long before the choice was clearly made... we had decided when choosing the motives" (Coreth, 1994, p. 99). To use a metaphor, the decision is already made by taking the train. The train then goes its course. We alone give the initial approval for a motive to determine and guide our volition and acts. The space where this takes place is not a space of nature and its determining forces, but rather a space of spirit, i.e. of freedom – as a uniquely human space. **Freedom** is, therefore, according to Coreth, **an essential element of human personal being**, who is (as specifically human) able to make responsible decisions and act morally.

Task:

Chose and carry out one of the three following tasks:

1. Write a philosophical-anthropological reflection (5-7 standard pages) on the movie, *The Truman Show* (Peter Weir, 1998), using relevant literature.
2. Write a philosophical paper (5-7 standard pages) on the topic, "Freedom or determinism?" using at least

three relevant philosophical sources. Express your stance and defend it by your reasoning in a discussion.

3. Using relevant literature, write a philosophical essay reflecting the issue of freedom on the basis of G. Orwell's book, *1984*, or on the basis of philosophical reflection on "The Grand Inquisitor" (part of F. M. Dostoevsky's novel, *The Brothers Karamazov*).

Print the paper and submit it in the following lesson.

Recommended literature:

(For recommended English sources consult your teacher)
CORETH, E.: Čo je člověk? Praha: Zvon, 1994, pp. 89 – 125.
LETZ, J.: *Filozofická antropológia*. Trnava: FF TU, pp. 80 – 110.
SARTRE, J.-P.: *Existencializmus je humanizmus*. Praha: Vyšehrad, 1996.[10]

---

10 CORETH, E.: Was ist der Mensch?: Grundzüge einer philosophischen Anthropologie. Innsbruck, Wien, München: Tyrolia 1973; SARTRE, J.-P.: *L'existentialisme est un Humanisme*, Éditions Nagel, Paris, 1946.

6. The Person and the Constitutive Dynamics of Interpersonal Relationships

the person – interpersonality – dynamic orientation – love – values

The term **person** was defined by E. Coreth as an "individual being of spiritual, thus conscious and free being experienced as *myself*" (Coreth, 1994, p. 153), specifically constituted through spiritual cognition, volition and action. The essence of a person is *constituted by personal relations*; thus, "to be a person means to be existentially oriented to the personal being of another" (Coreth, p. 155). M. Buber qualified a person simply as an accomplishment of a personal relationship You – I[11] (Buber, 1997); J. Sokol just mentions that a "person is established and maintained where there are personal relationships" (Sokol, 2002, p. 15). On the same basis of a substance-relational model of a person, S. Gálik formulates this integral definition: A human person is an "individual 'I'

---

11 BUBER, M.: Já a Ty. Praha: Kalich, 2005.

accomplished in conscious self-possessing and free self-disposing within relations with other persons" (Gálik, 2008, p. 124).

Perhaps the most important phenomenologist of the person, M. Scheler, defined the person as the centre of spiritual acts (Scheler, 1968, p. 66), while "spirit" is manifested *as* these acts and *through* them (spiritual love, cognition, compassion, etc.). "Person exists in and through spiritual acts" (Scheler, 1968, p. 74). M. Benköová notes that a person is, according to Scheler, inevitably "characterised as *unaccomplished*" as it is a "dynamic becoming, constant self-realisation" (Benköová, 2015, p. 61). Also in Scheler's opinion, the constitution of a person has always been taking place *already* within an interpersonal context, while loving is the most significant constitutive moment guiding a person toward reaching his or her deepest ontological possibilities. "On one hand, love is an act through which man reveals himself as the person, and on the other an act focusing on another person. Love constitutes the person as a centre of acts and is a peculiar ground of all acts. Its primacy has been found e.g. in knowing,[12] rational as well as volitional acts; it is the basis of any perception of values and a core of every preference (as a specific type of knowing val-

---

12 Compare SCHELER, M.: *Love and Knowledge*. In: SCHELER, M.: *Řád lásky*. Praha: Vyšehrad, 1971, pp. 5 – 34.

ues); it reveals its sense in moral orientation of a person (contrary to Kant's rigid formalism); it is the fundament of each interpersonal interaction, including sympathy. However, this does not mean that all acts could be reduced to love. Love is nevertheless the ground of all these acts, as it reveals the structure of man as person to the deepest possible extent."[13] (Benköová, 2015, p. 80; cf. also Luther, 1972, p. 103).

The above mentioned qualities and aspects of the notion of *person* indicate that the philosophical-anthropological search for the essence of man while focusing on maintaining the integrity of a human being leads to the accentuation of the term **interpersonality**.

From the etymologic point of view, the Latin word *persona* may be derived from Gr. "prosopon" composed of the prefix "pros" (to or towards) and "ops" (gen. opos), meaning face, eye or appearance. "Pros-opon" thus means "my face is turned towards something or someone" or "I am a counterpart of someone or something". The word refers to an immediate face-to-face relation-

---

[13] "Love is the deepest act accessible to man; it constitutes a human being as a specific person. As radically personal, that is – also unique, it is the basis of all other acts. It is not man as a man, but man as person, who loves." (Luther, 1972, p. 100)

ship. In light of etymology, person refers to the irreplaceable **uniqueness** and **relationality** of human reality, which has *always* and *already* been interpersonal (Yannaras, 2007, p. 5). Already the primary semantic content does not allow defining a person as an isolated static individuality (e.g. in the sense of Descartes' "cogito"). On the contrary, it always defines an individual within personal relations as a dynamic and creative orientation of an open, receptive and responsive unique individual life. The contemporary Greek philosopher, Christos Yannaras, who focuses on a person constituted by personal love (*eros*)[14] emphasises the priority of being-a-person over the search for essence. Similarly, the world of a man has always been *already* a personal world and our knowledge (of the world) has already been personal knowledge, i.e. it is never "neutral".

J. Sokol assumes another type of etymologic derivation. He derives the word *persona* from the Etruscan word for "mask" (mask of an actor, a role), implying the meaning of social or public identity or a role (Sokol, 2002, p. 18). Cicero says, a person has by nature two personas (roles,

---

[14] "This ecstatic self-transcendence necessarily refers to the fact of relationship. It is eros – as s a voluntary ascetic renunciation of atomic (existential and intellectual) self-sufficiency, as a perfect self-offering in love, always revealing the uniqueness and dissimilarity of circumstances of personal relationship" (Yannaras, 2007, p. XV).

natures) – one universal (as a human) and one unique (as an irreplaceable individual) (Sokol, 2002, p. 1p).

The first known definition of a person has been attributed to Boethius (480-524), who essentially defined a person as "Naturae rationalis individua substantia", i.e. an individual substance of a rational nature, or in other words, an "individual substance of the nature endowed with reason" (Sokol, 2002, p. 5). From an historical point of view, the term "person" and "personal" thus becomes related to the theological discussion regarding the Christian Trinitarian mystery. The term occurred with a new sense in the 4th century, e.g. with Gregory of Nyssa. The doctrine of the three divine persons of the Trinity became commonly used for expressing the existence of God who reveals Himself in this peculiar ways throughout history. The word "persona"[15] has been used for denoting God's individual hypostases. The hypostases acquired the meaning of Aristotle's first substance and Gregory of Nyssa thus took it for a synonym of "person" (Yannaras, 2007, p.16). Person as hypostasis is different from mere essence (nature) because of the *uniqueness* and *unlikeness* of qualities. It is rather an existential category, not an intellectual one; it precedes ontology and

---

15 Greek word "ousia" as essence, a substance; Greek "hypostasis" as an essential existence, individualised existence (Yannaras, 2007, p. 15).

may not be objectified; it is not part of the sphere of existence of the world's beings. At the same time, person has been defined by an essential dynamic relation to another person (similarly to the divine persons), by a loving participation in the existence of another person. **Person is a way of being of an individual existence, who actualizes himself or herself as a relation** (Yannaras, 2007, p. 18). This way is essential for the existence of a man as well; it is the sought essential "definition".

Even older theological connections may be genealogically revealed in Hebrew anthropology which was the first to refer to the dynamic substance-relational model of a human as a person. It is interesting that the Biblical view of a human has been somewhat "personal" since the very beginning – even in several senses: in the sense of the ontological *unity and integrity of a human creature* (e.g. the non-dualism of body and soul), in the sense of the *dynamic constitutive relationality* (dialogic relation, moral relation, the relation of love), or in the sense of the *unique irreplaceable identity and personal vocation* (the meaning of a "name" and "calling").

Biblical worldview has a personalistic as well as historical character. In the Book of Genesis, man as *Imago Dei* is described as the crown and purpose of all creation (Gn1, 1:31). In the first, earlier story of creation, God creates, because He freely wants – by the power of His words –

in six days ("Let there be light!"). Everything He creates has a highly positive value: "Then God saw everything that He had made, and indeed it was very good." (Gn 1:31) Thus, hereby we speak about positive anthropology, i.e. about anthropology characterized by a positive relationship to life and all creation (spiritual as well as material) – contrary to e.g. Gnostic or Platonic concepts refusing the material (and corporal) aspect of existence, considering it inferior or subordinate to spiritual reality exclusively understood as divine. In the following description of the creation of man (*ha adam*), humans were created from the dust of the earth and God's breath (spirit, *ruach*). Therefore, man is a being containing a unique fusion of material and spiritual being. "And the Lord God formed man of the dust of the ground, and breathed into his nostrils the breath of life; and man became a living being" (Gn 2:7). From an anthropologic point of view, it is important that the phrase "living being" or literally "a living soul"[16] (*Nefesh Chaya*) which man turned into at the moment of his creation, refers to the *whole of a living human being* – as a psychophysical unity (Tresmontant, 1998, p. 90), which is all permeated by the very breath of God, spirit (*ruach*) (Tresmontant, 1998, p.101). The spiritual is an integrated part of the physical (and

---

16 It is obvious that the Hebrew word for soul (nefesh) may not be identified with the Orphic-Platonic Greek term "psyche".

psychophysical); it is the mystery of God's presence in the very centre of His creation.[17]

"In the beginning, there is the relation", as Martin Buber writes in his work, *I and Thou* (Buber, 2005, p. 59). This sentence, reminiscent of The Gospel of John, may be easily situated in the biblical context of creation: man was *created as a relational being* and thus his essence has been originally defined by relationships to God and to other persons. Sin, interpreted as a violation of the interpersonal relationship of love between God and man, represents an imperfect way of existence of a man who departed from his or her original orientation of loving ("disobedience", "shame", "first fratricide", etc.). This relationship may be renewed in and through the loving relationships with others and with God, Loving Himself (Herself). This is the meaning of redemption and the very *core* of the teachings of three greatest monotheistic world religions, the religions of the so-called "Abrahamic tradition" (Judaism, Christianity and Islam).

Man is a historical being – in the sense of humankind as well as his or her individual history. He or she is existentially unaccomplished, opened toward the future,

---

17 "Hebrews had a great sense for physicality and love for her, precisely because they had a perfect sense for what is spiritual, for the presence of spirit within the physical" (Tresmontant, 1998, p. 99).

constantly "on the road", constantly being created in the process of his or her life. Man is an endless dynamic **self-transcendence**: "In Hebrew worldview, human existence is "exodus", i.e. going out (ex) to journey (hodos) somewhere else – through a desert to the Promised "Land". Thus, existence has been defined as the ever-present "beyond", exceeding the given "now" in its openness and self-transcendence (Balabán, 1996, p. 14). The Hebrew way of thinking brings the discovery and valorisation of **history** (expecting salvation or eschatological perspectives), the introduction of linear time contrary to the cyclical time of myths[18]; it is the thinking of events, motion, dynamics of free creativity and interactive relations. Man becomes a free co-creator of his or her life; he or she **chooses** (in contrast to the necessity of fate given in myths) and responds freely to the Deuteronomy call: "Choose life"[19]. He or she accepts full responsibility for his or her **moral decisions**. On one hand, *work* becomes toil and the human lot, on the other hand, it becomes the possibility of *creative* participation in creation, of developing activities enriching the world and the community.

---

18 Eliade mentions a mythical refusal of historicity and a fear to face the open uncertain future included in the historical perspective. "Just as the Greeks, in their myth of eternal return, sought to satisfy their metaphysical thirst for the "ontic" and the static, ... even so the primitive, by confirming the cyclic time idea" (Eliade, 2009, pp. 78 – 79).
19 Dt 30:15 – 20.

Eventually, in biblical anthropology, a personal relationship individualises and essentially brings man to himself or herself; this is also implied in the symbolism of the "name" and "calling". The Hebrew word, "hineni", meaning "Here I am", is an existential answer when one is addressed by his or her unique name in a face-to-face situation. Tresmontant wrote that biblical metaphysics is the metaphysics of *the name*. God calls a person individually and personally by his or her unique name, which is also an identification of a person in his or her own uniqueness and vocational situation. The biblical event of calling (*vocatio*) is granting identity in terms of individual vocation (*good-in-itself-for-me* – like in Scheler): "God wants and creates individual creatures for themselves; their individual identities are unique and irreplaceable" (Tresmontant, 1998, p. 94).

Viktor Emmanuel Frankl (1905-1997), a well-known Austrian neurologist and psychiatrist, who addressed also the philosophical questions of meaning and suffering on the basis of his own existential experience from Auschwitz[20], was also influenced by the ideas of such philosophers like M. Scheler, M. Buber or K. Jaspers. In his logotherapeutic practice, Frankl "applied" and "veri-

---

20 His famous book, *Saying Yes To Life In Spite Of Everything*. FRANKL, V. E.: *Napriek všetkému povedať životu áno*. Bratislava: Slovenský spisovateľ, 1998.

fied" the validity of many of the mentioned philosophical ideas. Therefore, we find his model of person worthy of attention and his ideas about the issue important – in terms of philosophical anthropology research as well.

Frankl refused any form of reductionism, considering them variants of nihilism; he distinguished three main types: physiologism as a reduction of a human being to his or her physical reality, sociologism as a reduction to social reality and its unavoidable influences, and psychologism as a reduction of a human being to his or her psychic states (Frankl, 2007, p. 11, p. 14-73). He also claimed the existence of a *spiritual dimension* of a human being, which is essentially *intentional, existential* and *personal*. As a spiritual being, a person searches for *meaning*. He or she does it in and through this three ways:

1) creative act, work, work of art (and correlative creative values)
2) fulfilling kinds of experience, deep personal relationships, mainly love (relational/interpersonal values)
3) turning suffering to performance (attitudinal values)[21].

Briefly, creativity–love–sacrifice are three spiritual events through which a person attributes meaning to

---

21 This technical-sounding formulation does not imply that Frankl wanted to introduce suffering as something positive (in the sense of personal performance). But he says that suf-

his or her existence. This meaning also constitutes and deepens oneself as a person (Frankl, 2010, pp. 29-30). According to Frankl, an individuated human being – as an integrated physical-psycho-spiritual unity – concentrates around and into a personal core which is his or her spiritual and existential centre. He even specifies the ontological structure of a human being by saying that rather than a personal core, it is a *personal axis*, going through all the surrounding psychophysical layers, including consciousness, pre-consciousness, unconsciousness. (Frankl, 2005, pp. 23-24).

Frankl defines the meaning of *person* in his ten interrelated theses (Frankl, 2010, p. 118):

1) The person as an *individual* is an undividable *unity*.
2) The person as *a unit* is irreducible to a greater unit (nation, race, state).
3) Every person as a spiritual being is an *absolute "novelty"* (perfectly unique and irreproducible).
4) The person may not be identified with the psychophysical organism; the person is *spiritual*. In comparison to person, an organism has an instrumental and

---

fering is the highest achievement a person is capable of, i.e. in the passivity of suffering that cannot be removed or mitigated, he or she still has an opportunity to take a spiritual stance of acceptance and turn it into a sacrifice in blind faith in some kind of attributed meaning (Frankl, 2013, pp. 83-85).

expressive function – the person acts and expresses him or herself through and as organism. This also means that a physical or mental illness does not detract from the uniqueness, interchangeability and dignity of a specific human person.

5) The person is *existential* – he or she does not belong to facticity; the person is *free*. The free choice is a privilege of a person, a following responsibility is his or her "burden".[22]

6) The person as autonomous and irreducible is part of an "I" dimension (contrary to "It"). A so-called "instinctual I" possessed by its drives is absurd and impossible in this sense. There is also "spiritual unconsciousness" – contrary to "instinctual unconsciousness" (dimension of "It"), which is the origin of the "unconscious religiosity" as well.[23]

7) The person founds and keeps the unity and wholeness of a physical-psycho-spiritual human being, who has always been oneness *already*. A spiritual per-

---

[22] "The person... is not determined by instincts; he is oriented towards meaning... He does not pursue pleasures, but values" (Frankl, 2010, p. 118).

[23] Instincts and instinctive determination would belong to the vital sphere – man as organism. On the contrary, freedom, responsibility, search for meaning and actualisation of values belong to the spiritual sphere – the sphere of the person. "Man is attracted by values, they do not press him" (Frankl, 2007, p. 38).

son is capable of a distant point of view regarding the psycho-physical dimension of his or her own being; he or she can observe and reflect himself or herself, and say "no" to his or her lower motives or drives.
8) A person is no static substance; it is rather a spiritual *dynamic and open* orientation.
9) For now it seems, that only a human may be called a person; animals lack "ex-centricity". Through the conscious relation to his or her being, a person is able to reflect or question a partial as well as holistic meaning of his or her existence.
10) The person always exists in relation to *the transcendence* and constitutes itself *as the person* through it. Thus, humans are (in a broad sense) religious beings, even though it would be just unconscious religiosity. The structure of the human person essentially assumes the withdrawal from "himself" and turning to what exceeds man (human You, divine You, destiny, universal love, higher meaning of the universe – no matter how veiled or vague, etc.) (Frankl, 2010, p. 118). "Man is, therefore, characterised by a phenomenon we consider essentially anthropological: the self-transcendence of human existence! By this I mean the fact that a human being always points above himself – to something he is not himself – to something or someone: to a meaning to be accomplished, or another human being he meets in love" (Frankl, 2013, p. 11).

The question of interpersonality as an essential constitutive element of the person is related to a peculiar understanding of the transcendence and the existentiality of a human being. We will illustrate this via Frankl's commentaries on a charming rabbinical story. The story portrays heaven and hell metaphorically; however, Frankl perceives them rather as the two existential orientations or states of a person. A righteous man came to the other world. First, he found himself in a dining room. There were many skinny, sad and moaning people sitting at a big table – yet there was a lot of delicious food on the table. In their hands, they had spoons almost three metres long, so they were not able to have even a small bite. But instead of feeding their neighbour sitting on the opposite side, they were sitting there hungry and unhappy. Contrarily, in heaven's dining room, there was joyful laughing and friendly talk accompanying the feast. Everyone was feeding his neighbour with his spoon and they were all satisfied and full. Frankl says: "The spoon is *intentionality*... You cannot direct your intentional act to yourself, only to something, which is not yourself. However, through reciprocity human existence becomes a possibility, because you are, I may say, a self-transcendence of another one."(Frankl, Lapide, 2005, p. 78).

In this sense, it is only possible to become a person through mutual interpersonal activity, focusing on one another. Similarly, Frankl mentions a personal self-realisation – a personal fulfilment and happiness: the direct way is doomed to frustration and failure, harrowing isolation (as in the story of the spoon). A man may only achieve the fullness and depth of his or her personal being indirectly; only indirectly – "accidentally he comes to self-accomplishment, personal fulfilment and happiness – by an *existential indirectness*, through the intentional focus on You".[24] The story reveals probably the greatest paradox of the autonomous existence of a human being. "When giving himself to a task to accomplish or to love another person, man actualises himself. The more he gives himself to his tasks, the more he gives himself to his partner, the more human he is, and the more he becomes himself. So he is able to fulfil himself only as much as he forgets himself, as he overlooks himself. Similarly, an eye is able to see, though this depends on it not seeing itself" (Frankl, 2013, p. 12).

---

[24] Frankl's dialogue partner, rabbi Pinchas Lapide, made the following comment on the existential "mechanism": "Man who lives and exists just for himself, it means, he is obsessed by his "self-performance", will eventually shrink, thicken and gradually die spiritually. 'I' he desperately adheres to, has been degenerating him into a cold and spiritless 'it', because his soul has been prevented from its ability to shine and influence the others, as requested by his true essence, be a free man who tries to rise above himself, inclines to another one and experiences his happy self-finding in a giving love" (Frankl, Lapide, 2005, p. 73).

Task:

Select and carry out one of the following tasks:

1. "The Person as the Transcendence" – write a philosophical-anthropological reflection (5-7 standard pages) on the movie, *Andrei Rublev* (Andrei Tarkovsky, 1966), using relevant philosophical literature.
2. Write a free philosophical reflection (5-7 standard pages) on the movie, *Persona* (I. Bergman, 1966), using appropriate philosophical literature.
3. Write a philosophical paper (5-7 standard pages) on "The Person According to Max Scheler" on the basis of a more thorough study of the primary and secondary literature.

Print the paper and submit it in the following lesson.

Recommended literature:

(For recommended English sources consult your teacher)
BUBER, M.: *Já a ty*. Praha: Kalich, 2005.
BUBER, M.: *Problém člověka*. Praha: Kalich, 1997.
FRANKL, V. E.: *Trpiaci človek*. Bratislava: Lúč, 2007.[25]
TRESMONTANT, C.: *Bible a antická tradice*. Praha: Vyšehrad, 1998., pp. 83 – 134.

---

25 BUBER, M.: *Das Problem des Menschen*. Gütersloher Verlagshaus; Auflage, 2001; *Ich und Du*. Gütersloher Verlagshaus; Auflage, 1999; TRESMONTANT, C.: *Essai sur la pensée hébraïque*, éd. O.E.I.L., 1953 (réédition 1956); FRANKL, V. E.: *Der leidende Mensch. Anthropologische Grundlagen der Psychotherapie*. Huber, Bern, 1975–2005.

7. Appendix: Short Exercise Book and Closing Remarks

(Answering the questions here requires a thorough knowledge of the recommended literature)

1. Describe the age, subject, topics and methods of philosophical anthropology in the 20th century ("modern" philosophical anthropology).
2. Name the main representatives of modern philosophical anthropology; name their key works and sum up their philosophical intention briefly.
3. The primary forms of human self-interpretation – mythical and religious man.
4. Myth as a symbolic form according to E. Cassirer.
5. Explain the relationship between spirit and life in Scheler's work, *The Human Place in the Cosmos*. What does his "sublimatory" solution consist of?
6. What is the meaning of Scheler's term "ideation"? Give examples.

7. How does Scheler understand "Deitas" and his relationship to man and the world?
8. The anthropological model of man in the biblical tradition.
9. What levels of "the psychic" (vital principles) does Scheler identify in the order of vital being? Describe their basic characteristic features as well.
10. Describe the concept of "ex-centricity" and assign it to an author and his work.
11. Introduce the aspect of "spiritual cognition" of man according to Emerich Coreth and the three "elements" it has.
12. Name and describe the forms of knowledge according to Max Scheler.
13. Name and describe the philosophical-anthropological contribution of E. Cassirer: "animal symbolicum".
14. Look at the relation between knowledge – volition – freedom and morality according to E. Coreth. Explain the concepts of "fundamental freedom" and "virtual infinity".
15. Explain the relation between feelings (emotions) and values according to Max Scheler. Explain his notion of "the person". What is "ordo amoris"?
16. What is compatibilism? Give examples of such philosophical solutions of the question of freedom.
17. Introduce Frankl's model of man.
18. Explain the importance of culture in H. Plessner's

philosophical anthropology. What does "mediated immediacy" mean?
19. Explain the importance of technology in A. Gehlen's philosophical anthropology. Why does he consider it a part of the very human nature?
20. Explain the etymology and development of the concept of "the person" and define it as an existential category.
21. Describe the image of man in the thought of ancient Hebrew thought.
22. Look at Buber's understanding of interpersonality. What does his criticism of M. Scheler consist of?

We have introduced the fundamental topics and issues of philosophical anthropology and we have mentioned the authors that are influential in the field. A student (or a reader) may test his or her knowledge of the selected chapters of philosophical anthropology by answering the above mentioned questions; their role is to sum up the issue in the form of questions. There are many topics concerning philosophical anthropology research which would be worthy of special attention and space, and we have not included and dealt with all of them here. Each of them has their specific problem fields, philosophical solutions and implications. These are, for example, how to find and qualify the human "essence" or the discussion on the essential definition of man; the well-known issue of psycho-physical dualism and the dualism of the spiritual and material in human existence (mind-body problem); or the issue of the final destination of man – death or possibly immortality (Letz, 2011); the issue of individual personal identity; evolution and creation; search for the meaning of human being, etc. We also could have focused on other authors who contributed or have contributed to the explanation of the philosophical and anthropological problems of man (K. Lorenz, C. Lévi-Strauss, existentialists, etc.). Questions we can pose within the field of philosophical anthropology are innumerable. Today, philosophical anthropology is as up-to-date as it was in the times of Max Scheler. No doubt, the question *What is man?* remains inexhaustible for both scientific and philosophical research.

Bibliography

AGASSI, J.: *Towards a Rational Philosophical Anthropology*. The Hague: Martinus Nijhoff, 1977.
BALABÁN, M.: *Hebrejské člověkosloví*. Praha : Herrman a synové, 1996.
BENKÖOVÁ, M.: K fenomenológii osoby Maxa Schelera. In: TRAJTELOVÁ, J. – BENKÖOVÁ, M.: *Od intersubjektivity k interpersonalite*. Trnava: Filozofická fakulta TU, 2015.
BUBER, M.: *Já a ty*. Praha: Kalich, 2005.
BUBER, M.: *Problém člověka*. Praha: Kalich, 1997.
CASSIRER, E.: *Esej o člověku*. Bratislava: Pravda, 1977.
CASSIRER, E: *Filozofia symbolických foriem*. Praha: Oikoymenh, 1996.
CORETH, E.: *Co je člověk?* Praha: Zvon, 1994.
ELIADE, M.: *Mýtus o věčném návratu*. Praha: Oikoymenh, 2009.
FRANKL, V. E. – LAPIDE, P.: *Hľadanie Boha a otázka zmyslu*. Bratislava: Lúč, 2009.
FRANKL, V. E.: *A přesto říci životu ano*. Kostelní Vydří: Karmelitánské nakladatelství, 2006.
FRANKL, V. E.: *Neuvedomený Boh*. Bratislava: Lúč, 2005.
FRANKL, V. E.: *Utrpenie z nezmyselného života*. Bratislava: Lúč, 2013.
FRANKL, V. E.: *Trpiaci človek*. Bratislava: Lúč, 2007.
FRANKL, V. E.: *Vôľa k zmyslu*. Bratislava: Lúč, 2010.
GÁLIK, S.: *Filozofická antropológia*. Bratislava: Iris, 2008.

GEHLEN, A.: *Duch ve světe techniky*. Praha: Svoboda, 1972, s. 29 – 47.
HODOVSKÝ, I.: Max Scheler – filosof ducha a citu. In: SCHELER, M.: *Můj filosofický pohled na svět*. Praha: Vyšehrad, 2003, s. 9-103.
HUSSERL, E.: *Krize evropských věd a transcendentální fenomenologie*. Praha: Academia, 1996.
KANOVSKÝ, M.: *Kultúra a sociálna antropológia. Osobnosti a teórie*. Bratislava: Chronos, 2004.
KOWALCZYK, S.: *An Outline of the Philosophical ANthropology*. Peter Lang, 1991.
LANDMANN, M.: *Philosophische Antropologie: Menschliche Selbstdarstellung in Geschichte und Gegenwart*. Berlin, 1982.
LETZ, J.: *Filozofická antropológia*. Bratislava: Charis, 1994.
LÉVINAS, E.: *Totalita a nekonečno*. Praha. Oikoymenh, 1997.
LORENZ, K.: Osm smrtelných hříchů. In: BLECHA, I. (ed.): *Filosofická čítanka*. Olomouc: Nakladatelství Olomouc, 2000, s. 464-469.
LUTHER, A. R.: The Articulated Unity of Being in Scheler's Phenomenology. Basic Drive and Spirit. In: FRINGS, M. S. (ed.): *Max Scheler (1974 – 1928). Centennial Essays*. The Hague: Martinus Nijhof, 1974, s. 1 – 42.
LUTHER, A. R.: *Persons in Love. A Study of Max Scheler's Wesen und Formen der Sympathie*. The Hague: Martinus Nijhoff, 1972.
MARCEL, G.: Člověk jako problém. In: BENDLOVÁ, P.: *Hodnoty v existenciální filosofii Gabriela Marcela*. Praha: Academia, 2003, s. 79 – 131.
MIRANDOLA della, P.: O dôstojnosti človeka. In: SEILEROVÁ, B.: *O dôstojnosti človeka. Odkaz Giovanniho Pica della Mirandola*. Bratislava: Iris, 1999.
PALMER, D.: *Does the center hold? In introduction to Western philosophy*. NY: The McGraw-Hill Companiess, Inc., 2008.
PASCAL, B. *Myšlenky*. Praha: Odeon, 1973.
PATOČKA, J.: Max Scheler. Pokus celkové charakteristiky. In: SCHELER, M. *Místo člověka v kosmu*. Praha: Academia. 1968, s. 5 – 41.
PLESSNER, H.: Člověk jako živá bytost. In: BLECHA, I. (ed.): *Filosofická čítanka*. Olomouc: Nakladatelství Olomouc, 2000, s. 446 – 449.
RÖD, W. – HOLZHEY, H.: Filosofická antropologie. In: *Filosofie 19. a 20. storočia II*. Praha: Oikoymenh, 2006, s. 287 – 322.
SARTRE, J.: *Existencializmus je humanizmus*. Praha: Vyšehrad, 1996.
SEILEROVÁ, B.: *Človek vo filozofickej antropológii*. Bratislava: Iris, 1995.

SCHELER, M.: *Formalism in Ethics and Non-Formal Ethics of Values*. Manfred S. Frings and Roger L. Funk (trs.), Evanston, IL: Northwestern University Press, 1973.
SCHELER, M.: *The Nature of Sympathy*. New Brunswick: Transaction Publishers, 2008.
SCHELER, M.: *Řád lásky*. Praha: Vyšehrad, 1971.
SCHELER, M.: *Místo člověka v kosmu*. Praha: Academia, 1968.
SCHELER, M.: *O studu*. Praha: Mladá fronta, 1993.
SCHELER, M.: *On the Eternal in Man*. Bernard Noble (tr.), London: SCM Press, 1960.
SCHELER, M.: *Můj filozofický pohled na svet*. Praha: Vyšehrad, 2003.
SKINNER, F.: *Beyond Freedom and Dignity*. Suffolk: The Chaucer Press, 1976.
SOKOL, J.: *Filosofická antropologie*. Praha: Portál, 2002.
SOKOL, J.: *Malá filosofie člověka. Slovník filosofických pojmů*. Praha: Vyšehrad, 2004.
SOUKUP, V.: *Teorie člověka a kultury*. Praha: Portál, 2011.
ŠLOSIAR, J.: *Od antropologizmu k filozofickej antropológii*. Bratislava: Iris, 2002.
TRESMONTANT, C.: *Bible a antická tradice*. Praha: Vyšehrad, 1998.
TRAJTELOVÁ, J.: *Kognitívna antropológia: Vybrané problémy*. Trnava: Filozofická fakulta Trnavskej univerzity, 2013.
TRAJTELOVÁ, J.: *Vzdialenosť a blízkosť mystiky*. Kraków/Trnava: Towarzystwo Słowaków w Polsce/Filozofická fakulta Trnavskej univerzity v Trnave, 2011.
YANNARAS, CH: *Person and Eros*. Brookline, Massachutsetts: Holy Cross Orthodox Press, 2007.
YANNARAS, CH: *Relational Ontology*. Brookline, Massachutsetts: Holy Cross Orthodox Press, 2011.
YANNARAS, CH.: *Variations on the Song of Songs*. Brookline, Massachutsetts: Holy Cross Orthodox Press, 2005.
ZVARÍK, M.: *Predsudok vo fenomenológii každodennosti*. Kraków/Trnava: Towarzystwo Słowaków w Polsce/Filozofická fakulta Trnavskej univerzity v Trnave, 2011.

Jana Trajtelová, PhD. works as a Scholarly Assistant at the Department of Philosophy, Faculty of Philosophy and Arts at Trnava University in Trnava, Slovakia. Her main areas of specialization are the Philosophy of Religion, and Phenomenology and Philosophical Anthropology. In 2011 she published a book on the phenomenology of mysticism, *Distance and Proximity of Mysticism: Phenomenological Study of Fundamental Movements in Traditional Western Mysticism* (2011), and is a co-author of the book *Person as Phenomenon: From Intersubjectivity to Interpersonality* (2015).

www.ingramcontent.com/pod-product-compliance
Ingram Content Group UK Ltd.
Pitfield, Milton Keynes, MK11 3LW, UK
UKHW021257180426
11947UKWH00015B/885